**W9-DEG-283**

NEW DIRECTIONS FOR HIGHER EDUCATION

Martin Kramer
*EDITOR-IN-CHIEF*

# Promising Practices in Recruitment, Remediation, and Retention

Gerald H. Gaither
*Prairie View A&M University, Texas A&M University System*

*EDITOR*

Number 108, Winter 1999

JOSSEY-BASS PUBLISHERS
San Francisco

PROMISING PRACTICES IN RECRUITMENT, REMEDIATION, AND RETENTION
*Gerald H. Gaither* (ed.)
New Directions for Higher Education, no. 108
Volume XXVII, Number 4
*Martin Kramer,* Editor-in-Chief

Microfilm copies of issues and articles are available in 16mm and 35mm,
as well as microfiche in 105mm, through University Microfilms Inc., 300
North Zeeb Road, Ann Arbor, Michigan 48106–1346.

ISSN 0271-0560          ISBN 0-7879-4860-8

NEW DIRECTIONS FOR HIGHER EDUCATION is part of The Jossey-Bass
Higher and Adult Education Series and is published quarterly by Jossey-
Bass Inc., Publishers, 350 Sansome Street, San Francisco, California
94104–1342. Periodicals postage paid at San Francisco, California, and at
additional mailing offices. Postmaster: Send address changes to New
Directions for Student Services, Jossey-Bass Inc., Publishers, 350 Sansome
Street, San Francisco, California 94104–1342.

SUBSCRIPTIONS cost $58.00 for individuals and $104.00 for institutions,
agencies, and libraries. See subscription order form at back of issue.

EDITORIAL CORRESPONDENCE should be sent to the Editor-in-Chief,
Martin Kramer, 2807 Shasta Road, Berkeley, California 94708-2011.

Cover photograph and random dot by Richard Blair/Color & Light ©
1990.

Jossey-Bass Web address: www.josseybass.com

Printed in the United States of America on acid-free recycled paper containing 100 percent recovered waste paper, of which at least 20 percent is
postcomsumer waste.

# CONTENTS

# EDITOR'S NOTES

The modern American system of mass higher education came of age in the years following World War II. To the classical concept of a liberally educated person, which more traditional and prewar elitist academic institutions had been developed to serve, was added an egalitarian impulse to extend educational opportunity to as many qualified aspirants as possible. Higher education now seemed capable of leading the uninitiated, the underserved, the disadvantaged, and the historically bypassed to play more elevated, useful, and active future roles in human affairs.

This new philosophy also seemed to have a higher aim: the systemic redemption of an educational and social system that had seemed incapable of rising above its elitist shortcomings without a concomitant change by the political system. There was an unwritten contractual agreement that those who benefited from higher education would compensate society in the future. If offering greater educational opportunity could alter a person's life to that of a more self-reliant citizen and gainfully employed taxpayer, the individual, the nation, and the national treasury would benefit. The enlightened professional educator and politician alike now jointly assumed a position of leadership, making and implementing new egalitarian education values for a new age.

These egalitarian changes had profound impacts on the college population. The GI Bill, the primary enrollment growth stimulus, also led to a more diverse student population. But as the number of students increased, there was a corresponding increase in the number of problems concerning student preparedness. Thus, one of the negative realities that gained prominence out of this new egalitarianism was a "decline in ability, displayed by students graduating from high school in the 1960's" (Cohen, 1998, p. 197). One contemporary study revealed that 95 percent of the freshmen who entered in the late 1950s lacked study skills, and two-thirds lacked reading skills (Markus and Zeitlin, 1992–1993). SAT scores manifested this lack of student preparedness. Among students taking the SAT in 1952, the Math score averaged 494; it increased to 502 in 1963 and then declined to 480 in 1975. A similar pattern was exhibited for the Verbal score: 476 in 1952, 478 in 1963, and 440 in 1975 (Cohen, 1998).

Educators attempting to explain this preparedness erosion pointed to a number of contributors: a decline in the quality of schools, television, disrespect for authority, single-parent households, school desegregation, social promotion, a reduction in the number of academic subjects taught, and others. The list and the debate still go on. But whatever the reason, more educational institutions began to offer remedial course work to entering freshmen. By 1981, 78.9 percent of four-year colleges and 83.8 percent of two-year colleges were offering tutorial or remedial programs. By 1991, the respective figures had jumped to 89.0 percent and 93.8 percent (Markus and Zeitlin, 1992–1993).

This pessimistic postwar fear of a national decline in standards and quality caused Americans to look backward and imagine a golden age of literacy before World War II. Alas, it appears such a time probably never existed. Colleges provided tutors in Greek and Latin as early as the seventeenth century. The first course in remediation was offered by the University of Wisconsin, Madison, in 1849. By the 1850s community colleges were being proposed as one means to relieve senior institutions of the "burden" of unprepared freshmen. Recruitment pressures at Harvard, Yale, and Columbia allowed underprepared students to enter in such numbers that by 1907, over half of their matriculated students failed to meet admission standards. Clearly, the remedial problem is hardly recent, and the facts dispel the notion that a golden age of education ever existed in the United States. Indeed, Chapters One and Six strongly suggest that remedial education will be an even greater component of the undergraduate curriculum in the new millennium.

Another common stereotype is that today's remedial students are underprepared recent high school graduates. Statistics from the Institute for Higher Education Policy (1998), however, found that more than one-quarter of the students are older than age thirty, and 46 percent of freshmen in remedial courses are older than age twenty-two.

What accounts for this seeming disconnect between the facts and the more gloomy misconceptions or stereotype? Many would argue that there is no disconnect and that we face a crisis of enormous proportion. Consider the California State University System, which draws its students from the top third of the state's high school seniors. In 1998, 54 percent of its freshmen failed the entry-level math test, and 47 percent failed the verbal exam (California Citizens Commission, 1999, p. 61). At the elite University of California System, 35 percent of the entering freshmen needed remedial courses in English proficiency (Estrich, 1998, p. 13A). It was the unpreparedness of students with exemplary high school grades and SAT scores that most seemed to shock the public. And nearly 10 percent of freshmen who attended Florida's public universities and colleges in 1998 on the state's Bright Futures Scholarships had to take remedial classes in reading, English, or math. Critics called the finding proof that this expensive program is not aiding Florida's best students.

Grade inflation in high schools is perhaps giving high achievers an unrealistic idea of their abilities. From 1987 to 1997, SAT scores fell 14 points, while the percentage of students with an A average taking the SAT increased from 28 to 37 percent (Sobel, 1998).

A segment of society and government is now questioning the quality or usefulness of publicly provided remedial education and the need or desirability to recruit students who need this help. Indeed, mass access to higher education—the egalitarian role of higher education in constituting a body of citizens, of producing and reproducing cultural life, of constituting the professions—is becoming viewed as "uneconomic" and outside the desired framework of public policy.

This situation has helped give rise to a growing importance of the culture of assessment and accountability in most state capitals and has built an important base for new methods of competition of public resources, more in line with normally accepted profit-centered efficiency criteria. From this new viewpoint, based on measurable inputs and outputs and cost sanctions, the growth of public funding for remedial education appears to be slowing. There has been a partial transfer to user-pays arrangements, with increased sentiments for full nonstate cost of recruiting, remediation, and retention systems growing, and a greater portion of tuition and fees paid for by undergraduates is looming.

There is as well a timidity toward resisting these trends. A 1997 survey by the State Higher Education Executive Officers shows that states are driving the move toward limiting funding for remediation at four-year colleges. Virginia, Nebraska, South Carolina, and Florida now prohibit remedial education, and Georgia, California, and Massachusetts have plans to reduce the number of remedial courses. Other states are addressing the issue by developing standards for high school graduates.

Paradoxically, while the fields of research and scholarship are becoming more diverse, the public notion of what makes a quality university seems to be growing narrower, more monocultural, more elite and less egalitarian, and more attuned to individual benefit rather than societal benefit. Governmental processes of standardization, such as performance funding, quality assurance, and performance indicators, tend to reinforce this effort, providing economic pressures to reshape educational institutions according to a reified and more prewar elitist model of the American university.

The chapters that follow address some of these problems that technological change, more diverse and expanding populations, and mass higher education have brought to the academy. These chapters also offer valuable clues to practical changes that need to be made.

In this issue of *New Directions for Higher Education* we explore how the rather staid and unexciting part of the education process—the supply chain, or the input and process segment—has become a very important piece in the success or failure of institutions. Throughout this volume, the chapter authors provide many exciting and "best practices" ideas. The agenda here is full: to understand growing diversity; to recognize that the problems are not going away, but that there are solutions; to see that philanthropy differs from charity in the shaping of public policy; and to realize that democracy rests on a faith in individual opportunity.

## Acknowledgments

I owe a special debt to Jeanette Williams, my staff assistant, and to Tony Adam, who served as my research assistant as well as a chapter author, for their patience, support, and attention to detail on this project. They are dedicated professionals who gave willingly of their time and experience so that the participating authors and I could gain maximum benefit from our scarcest commodity: time.

I thank the chapter authors for their contributions. All of them are busy professionals who are involved on a day-to-day basis with the topics they discussed. The intention from the start was to select experienced practitioner authors whose advice would provide the insight and practicality sometimes missing in nonpractitioners. They often had to overextend themselves, yet they remained civil about my many interruptions and short deadlines. They share my love of higher education and were dedicated to helping bring this volume to fruition.

Several funding sources helped prepare this issue, primary among them the Fund for the Improvement of Postsecondary Education. The patience and encouragement of my program officer, Frank Frankfort, deserves special recognition. The Kellogg Leadership Project and Rick Foster and Allen Jones provided seed money for the support of a related project that yielded valuable information for some chapters. Mike Nettles's chapter, with his colleagues, also secured assistance from the Pew Charitable Trusts and the United Negro College Fund. Martin Kramer, editor-in-chief of this series, provided patient encouragement. Finally, the comments of Roger Elliot, assistant commissioner of higher education of the Texas Higher Education Coordinating Board, inspired the issue title as well as the work itself. To all these agencies and people, I extend my heartfelt thanks.

Gerald H. Gaither
Editor

## References

California Citizens Commission on Higher Education. *Toward a State of Learning: California Higher Education in the Twenty-First Century.* Los Angeles: California Citizens Commission on Higher Education, 1999.

Cohen, A. M. *The Shaping of American Higher Education: Emergence and Growth of the Contemporary System.* San Francisco: Jossey-Bass, 1998.

Estrich, S. "It's Not Who Goes to College, It's Who Can Stay There." *USA Today,* May 12, 1998, p. 13A.

Institute for Higher Education Policy. *College Remediation: What It Is, What It Costs, What's at Stake.* Washington, D.C.: Institute for Higher Education Policy, 1998.

Markus, T., and Zeitlin, A. "Remediation in Higher Education: A 'New' Phenomenon?" *Community Review,* 1992–1993, *13,* 13–23.

National Center for Education Statistics. *Remedial Education at Higher Education Institutions in Fall, 1995.* Washington, D.C.: U.S. Department of Education, 1996.

Phipps, R. *College Remediation: What It Is, What It Costs, What's at Stake.* Institute for Higher Education Policy, 1998. Available online at http://www.ihep.com/remediation/pdf

Sobel, R. "The Problems with All Those A's." *U.S. News and World Report.* Aug. 31, 1998, 78.

*GERALD H. GAITHER is director of institutional effectiveness, research, and analysis at the Prairie View A&M University campus of the Texas A&M University System.*

1

*The college population of the United States will grow more slowly and unevenly geographically, and it will be older on average, increasingly more diverse, and likely less affluent. By midcentury a majority of the college population will be minorities, and all of the net increase in the college population will come from minorities.*

# Demographic Factors Affecting Higher Education in the United States in the Twenty-First Century

*Steve H. Murdock, Md. Nazrul Hoque*

Of the potentially significant changes in the U.S. population that will have an effect on future educational needs and services, three are among the most important relative to the magnitude of their potential impacts: the decline in the rate of population growth and changes in the sources of such growth, the aging of the population, and the increase in the number and proportion of minorities in the United States. These factors have been shown to have a marked impact on demographic, socioeconomic, and service factors (Murdock, 1995; Murdock and others, 1997).

## Demographic Trends

Although the U.S. population is growing at a rate that will lead to an approximately 10.5 percent growth in the population from 1990 to 2000, the general trend in population growth since 1960, as in other developed countries, has been one of decreasing rates of growth. In addition, under a wide variety of projection scenarios, future growth is likely to be slower, with the population projected to increase at a rate of less than 10 percent per decade from 2000 through 2050 (Day, 1996).

Coupled with slower growth is a change in the sources of that growth. National population change is a result of two mechanisms: natural increase (the excess of births over deaths) and immigration. U.S. population has historically increased primarily as a result of natural increase, with immigration accounting for more than 50 percent of total population growth only between 1900 and 1910. Immigration has played an increased role in the past several decades, however. From 1980 to 1990, the number of immigrants to the United States was 7.3 million, the largest in any decade since 1900 to 1910, accounting for 29.7 percent of the nation's net growth from 1980 to 1990 (Murdock, 1995); from 1990 to 1996, immigration is estimated to have been 5.6 million, accounting for 29.8 percent of U.S. population growth (U.S. Bureau of the Census, 1998a). These percentages attributable to immigration compare to 13.5 percent in the 1960s and 18.8 percent of growth in the 1970s.

**Origin.** The countries of origin of immigrants to the United States have changed dramatically during the past several decades. From 1820 (when the first immigration data were collected) through the 1960s, more than 50 percent of all immigrants were from Europe; by 1980 to 1990, only 10.4 percent were from Europe, while 47.1 percent were from Mexico and other parts of Latin and South America, and 37.3 percent were from Asia. In the 1990s, despite an increase in the number of immigrants from Europe, the dominance of non-European immigration has continued. From 1991 to 1996, Europe was the region of origin for 14.9 percent of immigrants to the United States, Mexico and Latin and South America accounted for 48.7 percent, and Asia was the region of origin for 30.5 percent of immigrants to the United States (U.S. Immigration and Naturalization Service, 1997).

**Age.** The U.S. population has aged significantly. In 1900, the median age of the population was 22.9 years; by 1990 it was 32.9 years. Whereas roughly 4.0 percent of the U.S. population was 65.0 years of age or older in 1900, by 1990 12.6 percent of the population was of that age. Because of the aging of the well-publicized baby boom generation (persons born between 1946 and 1964), who account for roughly 30 percent of the U.S. population, the median age of the population will continue to increase; by 2050 a median age of 38.1 years of age is expected, with 20.0 percent of all persons being 65.0 years of age or older (Murdock, 1995).

**Minority Populations.** Because of the increasing diversity of immigrants (Edmonston and Passel, 1994) and the higher birthrates of minority populations, the growth in minority populations has increased substantially. During the 1980s, non-Hispanic whites (Anglos) increased by 4.2 percent, the African American population increased by 12.0 percent, the Hispanic population by 53.1 percent, and the "other" population category (consisting of Asians and Pacific Islanders, American Indians, and others who are not of Hispanic origin) by 71.7 percent. Of the net population increase of 22.2 million in the United States from 1980 to 1990, 66.0 percent was accounted for by minority population growth. Between 1990 and 1997, it is estimated that the population increased by 18.9 million, with approximately 66.8 percent being due to minority population growth (U.S. Bureau of the Census, 1998b).

## Projected Patterns of Population Change

In examining projected patterns relative to each of the population factors noted above using U.S. Bureau of the Census projections, we emphasize the middle of several population projection scenarios provided in the most recent projections (Day, 1996). The middle scenario is the one most likely to characterize the future population of the United States.

The middle scenario projections assume that migration will average 820,000 per year throughout the projection period; this is a smaller number of immigrants than during the late 1980s and early 1990s but greater than the number in the first part of the 1980s. The Bureau of the Census also assumes that the total fertility rate will increase from 2.0 children per woman in 1995 to 2.2 children by 2050, due to the growth of minority and immigrant populations with higher levels of fertility, and that life expectancy will increase from 75.9 years in 1995 to 82.0 years by 2050. We use these projections with full realization of their limitations, but with the expectation, based on other analyses (Fosler, Alonso, Meyer, and Klein, 1990; Murdock, 1995), that although the exact number of persons projected to be in the future population is unlikely to be correct, the general trends are likely to be in the direction indicated.

There is no single most appropriate means of deriving mutually exclusive racial-ethnic groups or referring to racial-ethnic groups. We use the terms Anglo, black, Hispanic, and other, with Anglos defined as non-Hispanic persons of the white race, blacks as non-Hispanic persons of the black race, others as non-Hispanic persons of all other races (except the white and black races, so that the other racial-ethnic category includes non-Hispanic Asian and Pacific Islanders, American Indians, Alaskan Natives, and Aleuts and persons in an other racial group category), and Hispanics defined as Hispanics from all racial-ethnic groups. These categories were employed to produce values for which the sum across racial-ethnic groups is equal to the total population.

Finally, in examining the results we present, it is important to acknowledge that demography is not destiny (Murdock, 1995). A variety of social, economic, and other factors may have larger effects than demographic forces on higher education. Nevertheless, we believe that it is useful to examine the implications of such patterns for the future of higher education in the United States.

**Immigration.** The projections of the Bureau of the Census show a population of 393.9 million by 2050 and a likely average annual growth rate of 0.77 percent per year from 1990 to 2050. Projections suggest that 55 percent of the net growth in population is likely to be due to immigrants and their descendants (Day, 1996). As a result, immigrants will likely also play an increasing role in educational service utilization in the United States, exerting demands for a greater diversity of products and services.

**Aging.** The aging of the population base is expected to continue, with the population reaching a median age of 35.6 years by 2000 and 38.1 years by 2050. These changes will be reflected both numerically and proportionally among age groups. The proportion of the population less than 25.0 years of age is projected to decrease from 36.3 percent in 1990 to 33.6 percent in 2050, and the population of elderly persons, those 65.0 years of age or older, will increase from 12.6 percent in 1990 to 20.0 percent by 2050.

Substantial differences exist in the age structures of Anglo versus minority populations. For example, whereas 14.4 percent of the Anglo population was already 65.0 years of age or older in 1990, 25.0 percent will be 65.0 years of age or older under the middle scenario in 2050. Only 5.2 percent of the Hispanic population, 8.5 percent of the black, and 6.2 percent of the other populations were 65.0 years of age or older in 1990, and under the middle scenario only 14.3 percent of the Hispanic, 14.2 percent of the black, and 15.2 percent of the other population is projected to be elderly in 2050.

**Minority Increases.** The trend toward an increasing number and proportion of minority residents is also evident in these projections. Of the total net increase of 145.2 million persons projected to be added to the U.S. population between 1990 and 2050, 74.2 million are projected to be Hispanic, another 24.3 million are projected to be black, and persons in the other racial-ethnic group are projected to account for about 27.0 million of the total net increase. Thus, 86.5 percent of the net change in population is projected to be accounted for by members of minority groups. If these patterns continue, the proportion of the total U.S. population composed of Hispanics is expected to be 24.5 percent in 2050 compared to 9.0 percent in 1990; the proportion of blacks would increase from 11.7 percent in 1990 to 13.6 percent in 2050; and the proportion in the other racial-ethnic group (other than Anglo, black, and Hispanic) would increase from 3.6 percent in 1990 to 9.1 percent in 2050. The proportion of the total U.S. population composed of members of minority groups would be 47.2 percent in 2050 compared to 24.3 percent in 1990.

## Significance of Patterns of Population Change

The effects of current and future patterns of population change are both direct and obvious and indirect and subtle. First, slower rates of population growth point to slower growth in markets for all goods and services, including educational services. Thus, the declining rate of population growth is likely to lead to reduced rates of growth in the total number of potential students.

Equally important, the nature of that growth is likely to alter student characteristics markedly. The diversity of origins of immigrants coupled with faster rates of growth among minority populations is likely to lead to larger proportions of minority populations and students. Also, as the median age of the student population increases, the educational and retraining needs of older populations will need to be taken into account.

**Socioeconomic Changes.**  There will be changes in the socioeconomic characteristics of the population because of the differences that exist in the income and other resources of persons of different ages and racial-ethnic backgrounds. For example, in 1996, the median household income of households with a householder (head) 15 to 24 years of age was $21,438; it was $50,472 for a household with a householder 45 to 54, but $19,448 for a householder 65 years of age or older. Similarly, although the median household income in 1996 was $38,787 for households with an Anglo householder, it was only $23,482 for households with a black householder, and $24,906 for those with a Hispanic householder (U.S. Bureau of the Census, 1997). As a result, if changes do not occur in these socioeconomic differentials, the student population will tend to become older, more ethnically diverse, and poorer. An analysis of a similar set of projections (Murdock, 1995) in fact estimates that the average U.S. household in 2050 would have an income about $2,000 less (in 1990 constant dollars) in 2050 than in 1990 and that the percentage of families in poverty would increase by 3.0 percent if the socioeconomic differentials by age and race-ethnicity do not change.

**Enrollment Growth Rate.**  For higher education, such changes also suggest a substantial increase in the number of minority students. Day (1996) suggests that overall rates of growth in the number of college students are likely to be slower than in the past because of the aging of the population out of traditional college ages and the lower rates of participation of minorities in higher education, but the rates of growth in minority and older students will be substantial. Thus, the number of college students is projected to increase by only 2.9 million (20.8 percent) from 1990 to 2050. This is a rate of growth for sixty years that is only 3 percent greater than that for the 1980s and less than one-third of the rate of growth in enrollment for the 20-year period from 1970 to 1990.

**Future Student Characteristics.**  The characteristics of students will change dramatically from 1990 to 2050. The percentage of students who are Anglo will decline from 79.6 percent to 57.6 percent as the percentage of students who are Hispanic increases from 6.0 percent to 17.4 percent, the percentage that is African American increases from 10.0 percent to 13.0 percent, and the percentage who are members of other racial-ethnic groups increases from 4.4 percent in 1990 to 12.0 percent in 2050. Finally, all of the net increase in the college population would come from minority students because an absolute decline of nearly 1.4 million students is projected in the number of Anglo students over the projection period.

Day (1996) also suggests the growing importance of older students. Although the percentages by age are relatively constant over time because of the use of age-specific rates, an examination of the numerical changes underlying the proportions shows substantial increases in the number of older students. Thus, whereas the total population of students is projected to increase by only 20.8 percent from 1990 to 2050, the number of students 45 to 54 years of age is expected to increase by 57.3 percent, and the number 55 years of age or older is projected to increase by 136.9 percent. In addition, the underlying data suggest that from 1990 to 2050, 31.2 percent of the net increase in enrollment will be due to students 30 years of age or older. Clearly educational services will need to include those intended for older students. Overall, then, the demographic changes for the total population will be evident for the college population. The U.S. college population will grow more slowly, be older, and be increasingly diverse.

**Implications.** Decreased rates of growth suggest that the market for higher education services may decline. However, there will be substantial variability in growth patterns across the United States. Patterns from both the 1980s and the 1990s, for example, have shown much faster growth in the South and West than in the Northeast and Midwest, with the South and West accounting for 88.8 percent of net population growth in the United States in the 1980s and 80.9 percent from 1990 to 1998. Under conditions of slower growth, evaluations of geographic factors affecting the viability of institutions may come to play a larger role in the development of higher education institutions than in the past. Similarly, it may be necessary to plan the location of future colleges and universities carefully. Finally, although the growth rate in the United States and most other developed countries is projected to be relatively slow, many other parts of the world are expected to show substantial growth, increasing the growth in international student populations.

Age structure changes are likely to lead to decreases in the number of students of traditional college age and increases in the number of older students, and it is apparent that an increasing proportion will be minority students. To the extent that the mix of institutions reflects the needs of specific groups, shifts toward the growing segments of the population will be necessary. Similarly, if the socioeconomic resources of minorities do not change, it may be necessary to adjust to populations of students from families with more limited socioeconomic resources through the provision of increased levels of financial assistance.

Finally, it is obvious that because of immigration and patterns of natural increase, an increasing proportion of students will be minority population members. In fact, minority students represent the major source for the expansion of higher education markets. Figures 1.1 and 1.2 present a projection of the total number of students during each time period that would be enrolled in college assuming that the rates of enrollment for all minority groups were the same as those for Anglos in 1990. Although rapid rates of closure between Anglo and minority rates are unlikely to occur, such an event would have dramatic impact on total enrollment in higher education.

By 2050 total enrollment would be 20.3 million: 3.5 million more students than under the actual 1990 age and race-ethnicity-specific enrollment rates—and with a percentage increase from 1990 to 2050 of 46.2 percent, an increase similar to that which occurred in the 1970s. Clearly increases in minority enrollment represent an important factor for both improving the

**Figure 1.1.  U.S. College Enrollment, 1990 and Projected for 1998–2050, Using Alternative Enrollment Rates**

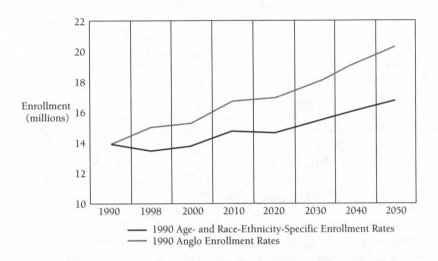

**Figure 1.2.  Projected Percentage of College Students by Race-Ethnicity for 2050, Using Alternative Enrollment Rates**

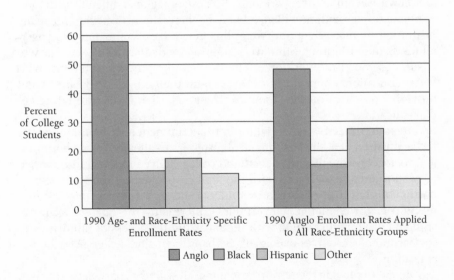

socioeconomic conditions of minorities and increasing the rate of growth in markets for higher education services. These projections also show that increased minority enrollment would markedly increase the proportion of both younger and minority students. Under the projections shown in Figure 1.2, by 2050, only 47.6 percent of all students would be Anglo; thus a majority of students would be of minority status. In addition, whereas 31.2 percent of the net increase in the number of students would be accounted for by students 30 years of age or older, the more extensive participation of minorities with younger age structures suggests that only 22.7 percent of the net increase would be attributed to such older students. Greater minority involvement would increase the number and proportion of traditional-age college students.

Overall, the demographics suggest that in the next century, growth in enrollment is likely to be slower and college students older and more diverse than in the past. Although these patterns in and of themselves are not problematic, the interrelationships that exist between such demographic characteristics as minority status and reduced access to socioeconomic resources are likely to make them challenging. Higher education will need to be more aggressive and more active in recruitment, retention, remediation, and fundraising. To ensure that the U.S. population is competitive in the international economy, its population must be well educated. It will thus be incumbent on higher education to take all steps possible to increase minority enrollment to fulfill its societal obligation and to provide the nation with a competitive workforce. Because of regional differences in rates of population growth, it will also likely be increasingly necessary for many institutions to increase minority enrollment as a means of maintaining overall levels of enrollment. Similarly, retaining students will be necessary to ensure a competitive workforce. This will require providing students with better educational opportunities throughout their educational careers and providing opportunities for them to strengthen their skills through remedial education.

**Resource Needs.**  Essential for both recruitment and retention will be the acquisition of additional financial resources to allow students with limited socioeconomic resources to attend college. Given recent trends, which have substantially increased both the total costs of education and the proportion of such costs absorbed by students and their families, this will represent a major challenge. Nevertheless, increasing the rates of minority student enrollment coupled with the more limited access of minorities to socioeconomic resources makes this perhaps the major challenge for higher education.

To fail to provide the resources to allow all segments of society to obtain higher levels of education would lead to reduced levels of education for the population as a whole when increased educational levels are likely to be necessary to manage increasingly sophisticated forms of technology. It would lead as well ultimately to a less well-educated and less competitive America. The future demographics of the United States thus suggest that meeting the challenges of higher education in the next century will be critical not only for higher education but for the nation as a whole.

## References

Day, J. C. *Population Projections of the United States by Age, Sex, Race, and Spanish Origin, 1995–2050*. Current Population Report, No. 1130. Washington, D.C.: U.S. Bureau of the Census, 1996.

Edmonston, B., and Passel, J. S. (eds.). *Immigration and Ethnicity: The Integration of America's Newest Arrivals*. Washington, D.C.: Urban Institute Press, 1994.

Fosler, R. S., Alonso, W., Meyer, J., and Klein, R. *Demographic Change and the American Future*. Pittsburgh: University of Pittsburgh Press, 1990.

Murdock, S. H. *An America Challenged: The Implications of Population Change for America's Future*. Boulder, Colo.: Westview Press, 1995.

Murdock, S. H., and others. *The Texas Challenge: Population Change and the Future of Texas*. College Station: Texas A&M University Press, 1997.

Pol, L. G., and Thomas, R. K. *The Demography of Health and Health Care*. New York: Plenum Press, 1992.

U.S. Bureau of the Census. *Money Income in the United States: 1996*. Current Population Reports. Washington, D.C.: U.S. Bureau of Census, 1997.

U.S. Bureau of the Census. *Estimates of the Population of States: Annual Time Series, July 1, 1990 to July 1, 1997*. Washington, D.C.: U.S. Bureau of the Census, 1998a.

U.S. Bureau of the Census. *Estimates of the Population by Age, Sex, Race, and Hispanic Origin: 1990 to 1997*. Washington, D.C.: U.S. Bureau of the Census, 1998b.

U.S. Immigration and Naturalization Service. *Statistical Yearbook of the Immigration and Naturalization Service*. Washington, D.C.: U.S. Government Printing Office, 1997.

*STEVE H. MURDOCK is a professor in and head of the Center for Demographic and Socioeconomic Research and Education, Department of Rural Sociology, Texas A&M University System.*

*MD. NAZRUL HOQUE is research scientist in the Center for Demographic and Socioeconomic Research and Education, Department of Rural Sociology, Texas A&M University System.*

2

*Recruiters in the future will place more emphasis on electronic media, student information systems, statistical technologies, and increased use of geodemographic tools, but the most important parts of new student recruitment will remain many of the traditional methods of nonprofit marketing used in recruiting.*

# Effective Admissions Recruitment

*Don Hossler*

There was a time when most college administrators and faculty believed that the only personal traits required to be an effective admissions counselor were a warm handshake and a friendly smile. In fact, effective new student recruitment has probably never been that easy, and in the current competitive environment, successful recruitment requires far more than simply good interpersonal skills. In the past two decades, there has been a growing emphasis on the use of applied social science techniques in admissions recruitment. In the late 1970s and early 1980s, college admissions professionals began to borrow concepts, ideas, and research techniques from the for-profit and not-for-profit marketing literature. The book *Marketing for Nonprofit Organizations* (Kotler, 1975) quickly became a primary resource for many admissions professionals. In 1983, Litten, Sullivan, and Brodigan coauthored *Applying Market Research in College Admissions,* in which they demonstrated how admissions recruitment efforts could be strengthened through the use of market research. Since these early source books, publications have appeared on topics ranging from the use of focus group research in college admissions (Bers, 1987), to handbooks on admissions marketing (Dehne, Brodigan, and Topping, 1991), to compendia of admissions recruitment strategies (Abrahamson and Hossler, 1990).

Every time an admissions office hires a new professional staff member, questions implicitly arise about the nature of effective admissions professionals. Is effective recruitment the result of interpersonal skills, knowledge of marketing practices, and research techniques? Or is it an art that relies heavily on instinct and experience? This chapter emphasizes the applied social science approach to admissions recruiting.

Research and a strong marketing plan are central to successful admissions recruiting because they enable the admissions staff to reach prospective

NEW DIRECTIONS FOR HIGHER EDUCATION, no. 108, Winter 1999  © Jossey-Bass Publishers

students when they are ready to make decisions about colleges. An analytical approach to admissions enables institutions to reach students when they are first considering broad types of colleges and which to apply to, or when they are starting to ask how they will pay for their education. The ability to segment prospective student markets and reach them with targeted, personalized information and recruitment activities is more important than the quality of the paper on which direct mail pieces are printed, the style and kind of information provided in these pieces, or the interpersonal skills of admissions professionals. An off-campus preview can be a powerful recruitment tool, but if the marketing plan is not developed and prospective students are informed too far in advance of the preview (in which case they might forget about the event) or too late (in which case they might already be busy on the day of the preview), then the success of preview events can be jeopardized. A sound plan and follow-up on the marketing plan are integral to successful recruitment.

Market research, geodemographic databases (such as the Enrollment Planning Service [EPS] or Predictor Plus, both available from the College Board, Educational Opportunity Service [EOS] from the American College Testing Service [ACT], or Forecast Plus developed by Noel-Levitz), and sound marketing principles provide the context for effective recruitment efforts. Admissions research and a marketing plan enable admissions professionals to understand the challenges they face in achieving their recruitment objectives. They also set the stage for implementing a successful recruitment effort.

This chapter looks at good practices that lead to effective new student recruitment. The primary focus is on the recruitment of recent high school graduates who are applying to a residential college.

Understanding the market position occupied by a college or university is the first step in developing an effective recruitment strategy. Highly selective private institutions with deep applicant pools and many prospective high-ability students will employ a different set of recruitment activities than will a regional nonselective public university. Many public flagship universities or second-tier private institutions find that they do not enroll the desired number of high-ability students (as often as they might wish) because they compete with national highly selective institutions, such as Princeton, Yale, Williams, or Stanford. Public flagships will similarly opt for a different mix of recruitment activities than will a small, less selective, regional private college. Understanding the context of the recruitment challenge for each individual college or university is a critical first step in determining the most effective recruitment activities.

## Stages of Recruitment

In addition to understanding the context of recruitment efforts, the stage of the recruitment process also determines the set of activities employed. The process of recruiting a new student can be broken down into several stages, but for simplicity, two main recruitment stages are focused on here: developing the applicant pool and converting applicants to enrolled students (matriculants).

**Developing the Applicant Pool.** The degree of institutional visibility is a critical part of building an applicant pool. As the size of an institution increases, the likelihood increases that prospective students and their families have heard about the school. The achievements of alumni or faculty, events sponsored on the campus, athletics, or music programs all play a part in broadening the visibility of a college or university. Institutional proximity also affects campus visibility. Size and proximity, however, tend to be static; there is little an admissions office can do to alter such campus characteristics.

The admissions office is charged with the primary responsibility for developing the applicant pool. Because greater institutional visibility results in more student responsiveness to recruitment efforts, an integrated marketing effort that uses the resources of the public relations staff and the office of admissions can help build a stronger applicant pool. This is especially important for less prominent regional public and private institutions. More important, print and electronic media provide some of the most effective methods for reaching prospective older and nontraditional students. Traditional-age prospective students are more likely to respond to such recruitment activities as direct mail, telemarketing, high school visits, and previews if they are familiar with the college or university. The use of print media, radio, and even television may be a prudent investment to enhance institutional visibility. These media tools also reach parents and local community opinion leaders. As parents, other family members, friends, and teachers begin to encourage college attendance, they often mention the names of specific colleges. This is part of the process of developing institutional visibility. A strategic integrated marketing plan can be part of the foundation of building a strong applicant pool. For traditional-age students, this is an ongoing process that is not tied to any specific months in the recruitment cycle.

During the past two decades, the recruitment process has started earlier and earlier. In 1975, Lewis and Morrison found that only 10 percent of high school seniors had started to request information about colleges they were considering in October of their senior year. By 1998, Hossler, Schmit, and Vesper reported that most students begin this process in the late spring or summer between their junior and senior years. They also found that most high school students are beginning their search four to five months earlier. Thus, it is incumbent on admissions offices to develop a series of recruitment strategies that are appropriate for ninth-grade students who are just starting to think about going to college as well as for second-semester seniors who may have applied and have been admitted to two or three different institutions. Indeed, even after submitting an enrollment deposit, some seniors are still shopping for colleges and could decide not to attend the school to which they have submitted an enrollment deposit. Therefore, a systematic recruitment plan includes many different types of direct mail, telemarketing, and off-campus previews; on-campus visitation events; and a variety of mechanisms for communicating the probable net price of attendance.

It is also important to call attention to the fact that increasingly ninth- and tenth-grade students are contacting colleges and universities and requesting information about the campus and major areas of study. At this early age, students (and their parents) are not likely to have very specific questions about institutions of higher education; they are still trying to sort out what kinds of colleges or universities in which they are most interested in attending. Many ninth and tenth graders do not yet understand the differences between research universities and liberal arts colleges; they do not fully understand what it means to live on campus or to commute from home; and they are not yet thinking much about the costs of college or student financial aid (although their parents are very interested in this topic) (Hossler, Schmit, and Vesper, 1998). For these younger students, direct mail is the most cost-effective way to keep them interested in a specific institution. Information should not be too detailed. It should be general and written for both students and their parents. Students and their parents, however, are becoming increasingly sophisticated consumers of college recruitment efforts, and colleges and universities should not have only one set of print material for ninth- and tenth-grade students. If a tenth-grade student receives print material that she also received in the ninth grade, it may have a negative effect.

**Converting the Applicant Pool.** Sometime during the junior year or the summer between the junior and senior years, most college-bound students become more focused about the college decision-making process. They begin to request college application materials and submit applications. The dilemma for admissions officers is that they never know when precisely each individual student has made this transition. This is not a trivial issue. Cumulative research (of which there is little) and conventional wisdom (of which there is more) suggest that when an admissions office reaches a junior who is ready to begin a more serious exploration of colleges, these campuses will have a competitive advantage in moving the student from a prospect to an applicant. However, if these efforts start before they make this transition, prospective students are less likely to read or respond to more detailed print materials or other recruitment activities. Most prospective students apply sometime between the summer of their junior year and the fall of their senior year (Hossler, Schmit, and Vesper, 1998). They have spent the summer and early fall eliminating colleges they are no longer considering and drawing up the list of colleges and universities to which they will apply.

Once students have reached the readiness stage of rising junior and move into senior status, an integrated recruitment effort designed to move students from applicants to matriculants should be put into place. A plan should include direct mail, e-mail, the Web, telemarketing, previews, and on-campus recruiting events. Abrahamson and Hossler (1990) have delineated a range of recruitment activities: print publications, advertising publications, college-generated publications, network marketing (marketing to high school counselors, high school faculty, alumni, and parents), direct mail, videotapes, radio and television, telemarketing, marketing in the field (high school visits, college fairs, and hotel programs), and on-campus programming and activities.

One of the advantages of differentiating between recruitment strategies to develop and convert the applicant pool is that they provide conceptual frameworks for organizing a diverse set of activities for admissions staff. Perhaps more important, it also provides a way of communicating roles for campus offices (such as public relations and residence life) and faculty and academic departments. For example, when prospective students are ready to determine which college they will attend, they become highly interested in gaining detailed information about academic programs and social life on campuses. Campus visits and opportunities to visit with faculty or learn more from student affairs staff become important parts of the conversion process. Admissions personnel need to communicate to faculty and campus administrators that the admissions office should be the expert in developing the applicant, but that once prospective students are ready to apply, the faculty, student affairs, and other campus representatives can play a key role in converting the applicant pool.

## The Role of Financial Aid

During the past fifteen years, colleges and universities have increasingly competed not only on the basis of quality, academic programs, and tuition costs but also on the basis of financial aid. Multivariate analyses are used to determine the optimal level of financial aid awards to students with desired academic traits or other personal attributes in order to enroll more of these students.

The use of logistic regression and other statistical techniques to determine merit and need-based campus financial aid strategies enables admissions offices to inform prospective students and their families about potential and actual campus financial aid awards. To use campus-based aid effectively, admissions personnel must seek ways to inform students as early as possible in the recruitment process. Here too timing is crucial. Traditionally, financial aid has been viewed as a way to help convert students who have already applied. However, financial aid information can also influence a student's decision to apply or to finish an incomplete application. As college costs have risen, students and parents are increasingly concerned about the net cost of college attendance. Students drop and add potential colleges and universities to their consideration sets on the basis of incomplete information on the net cost of attendance. Early knowledge of a potential financial aid award because of academic performance in high school or special music talent may influence a student's decision to apply. As a result, the task for admissions officers is to find the most effective ways to communicate potential campus scholarships as well as actual awards (after a student is admitted and a complete financial aid package has been constructed). Direct mail and telemarketing can be effective approaches for informing students of potential awards and later, actual awards.

## Guiding Principles

Two principles should guide all recruitment activities: personalization and timing.

**Personalization.** The more personalized an admissions office can make the admissions process, the more positive the response will be from students. Dehne, Brodigan, and Topping (1991) note that higher education is an intangible product. As such, the more it can be personalized during the recruitment process, the more effective the marketing efforts are likely to be. In direct mail, telemarketing, campus visits, and all other forms of recruitment, students view the level of personalization as a form of courtship. It is a way for campuses to let students know that "we would like to have you join us and spend some time here."

Anderson (1994) rated the effectiveness of direct mail recruitment activities of several large public universities. She reported that the degree of variation of personalization among these institutions was one of the most prominent differences in their direct mail recruitment efforts. Personalization is also important in telemarketing. As sophisticated telemarketing software packages have become available, admissions staff can now review the kinds of communications the office has already had with a student or parent. These new systems make it easy to store and retrieve information on a student's family or what instrument a student plays so that telemarketers can personalize every telephone interaction. In addition to a foundation of market research and a marketing plan, successful recruitment efforts often hinge on timing and personalization.

**Timing.** By focusing on timing, institutions should strive to reach students when they are ready for information. For too long, too many institutions of higher education, especially public institutions, were more likely to recruit prospective students when it was convenient for them rather than trying to match their behaviors to the readiness stage of students. Timing is also important from another perspective. As Litten (1986) noted several years ago, choosing colleges is a "risky decision" for families and one for which the students have had no previous practice. The sooner an admissions office can provide information, turn around an admissions decision after an application has been submitted, or determine the amount of a financial aid award, the more likely it is that a prospective student will respond favorably to recruitment efforts. Colleges and universities can ill afford to plan their recruitment efforts around what is best for the campus rather than being responsive to the timing needs of students. The optimal goal for admissions personnel is to provide information for prospects at just the right time so as to keep them interested in their respective institutions.

Trying to reach prospective students at times when they are at a readiness point for information or to take another step in the college choice process should be a central part of a marketing plan (Gallotti and Mark, 1994). There are several reviews of research on the college choice process as well as a recent book chronicling this process for a group of nearly five thousand high school students in Indiana (Hossler, Braxton, and Coopersmith, 1989; Hossler, Schmit, and Vesper, 1998; Kappler, 1998; Paulsen, 1991). These sources all agree that a pattern emerges for the timing of the college choice process among traditional-age students.

*Sophomore and Junior Years*

1. Sophomores who plan to attend a college or university after high school begin to form a list of schools they might consider attending. Most do not yet actively seek or read information about colleges. Parents and friends are still their primary information sources.
2. Parents of sophomores start to become concerned about college costs, and many start to seek out more information about financial aid and college costs.
3. Throughout their junior year, students begin to broaden the kinds of characteristics they are looking for in the institutions they consider. They also begin to add and drop colleges from their consideration set.
4. As juniors, especially second-semester juniors, students begin to seek out and read information about colleges and universities. Students with higher grades in high school tend to start this process earlier in their junior year. They seek information from friends, teachers, counselors, and family members, and they study written information from colleges and universities.
5. Juniors begin to take the SAT and ACT, which become trigger events in terms of thinking more about their college choice decision.
6. Many juniors make their first campus visit in the late spring or in the summer between their junior and senior years.

These findings indicate that marketing and recruitment resources directed to high school sophomores should be selectively restricted. Direct mail pieces should be succinct and written as much for parents as for prospective students. During the junior year, students are ready for more detailed information from admissions offices. They may also be ready to visit campuses or attend previews hosted in locations near their home towns. The summer months are increasingly becoming a good time for both of these activities. Parents are very interested in specific information about college costs and the possibility of scholarships.

*Senior Year*

1. Student information-gathering activities reach their peak in the fall of the senior year. One of the results may be information overload.
2. Peers, teachers, counselors, and admissions offices become primary sources of information about colleges; the role of parents begins to recede.
3. During the fall, students finally start to become interested in college costs and financial aid information.
4. Most students have applied by January.
5. After January, few students add new colleges to their consideration set.
6. The consideration sets of colleges that students evaluate become more realistic. Students begin to rate more highly campuses that are less costly and closer to home.

By the fall of the senior year, seniors are simultaneously very active in seeking out information about colleges and universities and more likely to report that they are feeling overwhelmed by the amount of information. Furthermore, they often report that they are no longer reading everything they receive or reading everything carefully. This information reinforces the idea that the spring and summer of the junior year are becoming a better time to reach prospective students. Since students are now more interested in college costs and scholarships, information about a possible scholarship or an awarded scholarship that is communicated during the fall may have an impact on students' decisions about where to apply or even where to attend. Most students have stopped adding any previously unconsidered colleges by January. Thus, sending search direct mail pieces out to students for the first time is no longer productive.

## Getting Ready to Recruit

Nearly twenty-five years ago I was talking with a colleague in admissions. He was worried because a member of his staff had been to a particular high school only once this year. I asked if the number of visits seemed to make a difference. He responded that his institution seemed to get fifteen to twenty students from this high school every year no matter what the office did, but since he did not really know what recruitment activities made a difference, he was hesitant to change anything.

Just as the awarding of campus-based financial aid has become more strategic, relying on multivariate analyses to determine amounts of awards, so have recruitment activities become more data driven. Determining how favorably prospective students respond to view books and how they rate the quality of campus visits determine in part the ultimate success of recruitment efforts.

Colleges and universities now trim or expand their recruitment territories on the basis of geodemographic analysis. If admissions recruitment is to be efficient and effective, the director of admissions must be able to answer the following questions:

Have there been increases or decreases in the number of high school graduates from the high schools and regions where we are attracting our prospects, applicants, and matriculants? If there have been changes, have they come about because of a shift in the number of seventeen- and eighteen-year-old students or a change in the number of students dropping out of high school?

Are there regions where we currently do not recruit but for which the characteristics of the population base are similar to other territories where we are recruiting very successfully? If the answer is yes, this may be a good area in which to expand recruitment efforts. Geodemographic tools such as the Enrollment Planning Service from the College Board and the ACT product PRIZM can enable admissions offices to focus efforts where they are most likely to be successful.

Multivariate analysis is also being used to determine the effectiveness of recruitment efforts. New student information databases enable admissions offices to store and retrieve background information about students easily and also record every type of recruitment activity and other forms of contact between student and institution that each prospective student has experienced. Using logistic regression, it is then possible to identify the types of recruitment activities that are most highly correlated with subsequent decisions to apply and enroll.

For example, recent analyses conducted at Indiana University reveal that we are more likely to enroll students who are first referred to us by alumni, teachers, friends, and others. We have also learned that students who initiate contact with us by e-mail are more likely to enroll. These insights enable us to direct more attention and resources to students who have been referred and those who contact us by e-mail. Similar analyses conducted at a private liberal arts college revealed that students who applied for financial aid were more likely to matriculate than those who had not. The institution is using this information, along with other indicators, to trim its mailing lists during the second-semester recruitment cycle in order to reduce costs.

Ongoing evaluation is important in all areas. Admissions print material should be evaluated by prospective students every two to three years. In 1998 marketing experts from the Office of the Vice President for Public and Governmental Relations at Indiana University conducted an extensive study of how prospective students responded to the admissions view book. As a result, the view book has been altered dramatically. It has fewer pages, it is crisper, and it has more photos and student testimonials; it also cost $40,000 less to print and is less costly to mail. An ideal outcome for an admissions office is something that works better and costs less.

It is always more exciting to look for the new innovation that will transform the effectiveness of an admissions office. Sometimes these creative insights do come along, but in most instances a sound marketing plan along with excellent follow-through and ongoing evaluation of recruitment activities will prove the most direct path to success.

## New Developments in Admissions Recruitment

Direct mail, high school visits, college fairs, telemarketing, off-campus previews, alumni recruitment, and on-campus visits remain the mainstay of admissions recruitment. Admissions professionals should be constantly striving to improve these activities. Geodemographic tools can enable admissions professionals to refine the regions of the country where colleges send direct mail recruitment pieces. Admissions professionals are constantly striving to enhance on-campus visitation programs by involving faculty more, providing "red-carpet" tours of campus facilities, or offering individual or small group financial aid counseling as part of a campus visit. An effort to strengthen existing recruitment activities is always a wise strategy. In addition, several new activities and approaches to student recruitment are emerging.

**Electronic Media.** CD-ROMS have become a popular recruitment device. The quality of CDs ranges from view books, catalogues, and video clips that can be viewed in a linear fashion. Highly interactive CDs have also been developed; they enable students to create customized virtual tours of a college campus as well as to explore the kind of detailed information that might be found in college catalogues. The emergence of the Internet has also created additional vehicles for student recruitment. Some observers of the college admissions process argue that the emergence of the Internet has already made CD-ROMS obsolete. That may eventually be true, but many colleges and universities continue to invest in this technology. Highly interactive CDs may continue to have a role until the bandwidth of the Internet expands and more homes have high-speed modems. For the moment, interactive CDs with multiple links to campus Internet sites can serve as a "table of contents," engaging prospective students, until the capabilities of the Web become available to more homes.

The new generation of student information systems being installed on college campuses stores e-mail addresses along with street addresses and telephone numbers. As a result, it is possible to communicate directly with students and parents via e-mail. This offers the possibility of lower costs, more frequent communication, and more personalized recruitment. Many colleges are looking into e-mail management systems that would recognize key words in students' e-mail requests and automatically construct appropriate electronic responses to queries as well as provide direct links to Web pages that provide further information. With respect to e-mail, all institutions have learned they need to assemble an e-mail library that can be used to address frequently asked questions.

The Internet allows the use the World Wide Web as a recruitment tool. The Internet can provide all of the print information currently available in view books, college catalogues, class bulletins, financial aid brochures, and so forth. As the bandwidth of the Internet expands and the speed and memory of home computers continue to increase, cost-effective videos will also soon be available.

The question remains of how to use the Web most effectively in outreach-oriented phases of admissions recruitment. The Web is frequently viewed as a passive medium for college admissions in the sense that prospective students have to seek out the sites of colleges and universities. For smaller and less well-known institutions, this makes the Web a potential problem; if students do not visit their Web sites, the site has less value. Precisely how students use the Web in gathering information about colleges and universities remains unknown. A recent study (Strauss, 1998) indicates that most students are not yet relying on the Web as a primary source of information. Rothschild (1998) conducted a less formal but insightful study of how prospective students use the Web. He found that students reported browsing the Web for general information about colleges and universities in the early stages of their college search process. Once they had narrowed their search down to the final set of two or three institutions, students started looking for detailed information about academic programs, student life, and financial aid. These insights should give all admissions offices pause because the Web is still democratized and decentralized on many campuses. The quality of departmental and student affairs Web sites varies widely and indeed, such differences in quality may not exist at all. This could create a negative impression.

The Web has the greatest potential for an immediate impact by rapidly expanding the levels of personalized service for prospective and currently enrolled students. Many students (and parents) are anxious to know if all of their application material has been received by the colleges and universities to which they have applied. Others want to know the status of their financial aid application. Admissions offices are increasingly using the Web to enable students to apply electronically and to allow applicants to look up their application status or their financial aid status on a secure Web account. Using the Web for student applications and to check on the status of an admission or financial aid application provides the kind of personalized services that families increasingly expect. In addition, the Web can reduce the amount of staff time spent on data entry and answering telephone calls from anxious prospective students and parents.

**Telemarketing.** One way to personalize recruitment is by telephone. Admissions staff have been using the telephone to contact prospective students for more than twenty years. More recently, the use of the telephone has become a form of telemarketing designed to help admissions staffs make more strategic decisions. Most admissions offices hire teams of current students who use student information systems and scripts to track the interests of students. Telemarketing can be used to help determine whether students on an institution's prospect list are really interested in receiving additional information about the campus. It can be used later in the admissions cycle to determine whether an admissions staff member should continue to work with an applied or admitted student who has since eliminated the college or university from further consideration. Telemarketing can be used to invite students to off-campus or on-campus events, inform them they have been admitted, and tell them they have received a scholarship. Many of these tele-marketing strategies are not new, but telemarketing information systems and the degree to which student responses determine additional marketing inter-ventions prospective students might receive is new. Another development is the emergence of third-party vendors, such as Ruffalo Cody, which man-age and often execute critical phases of telemarketing efforts for many insti-tutions.

**Off-Campus Recruitment.** High school visits and college fairs have been a mainstay of campuses for decades, although a number of factors are chang-ing these standard efforts. Some small colleges are finding that too few students attend their high school visitations to justify the staff time. The statistical analy-ses and evaluations of the recruitment activities conducted by some institu-tions have revealed that high school visits and college fairs have little impact on the college choice process of students in their prospect or applicant pools. In addition, high schools increasingly limit the amount of time students can spend attending presentations made by admissions counselors.

For all of these reasons, off-campus receptions and previews held in hotels, homes of alumni, or offices of alumni are growing in popularity. Sta-tistical analyses and evaluation studies often find these activities are suc-cessful. Off-campus previews enable institutions to invite prospective students from a geographical region to hear presentations by an admissions counselor and currently enrolled students who may have graduated from a nearby high school. In addition, one or more faculty members and success-ful, well-known alumni who reside in the area can make presentations. These previews enable admissions offices to focus significant amounts of resources on audiences who are likely to be receptive.

**Integrated Recruitment Efforts.** The concept of enrollment manage-ment is increasingly being used on college and university campuses to orga-nize and integrate the activities of nonacademic and academic units to achieve enrollment objectives. Not surprisingly, the enrollment management framework is bringing more campus offices into the admissions recruitment process. Increasingly, high school students apply to more institutions than they did in the past and also make enrollment deposits to more than one campus. Admissions and enrollment management professionals have come to the realization that recruitment does not stop with the receipt of an enrollment deposit. No one knows precisely how many students forfeit their deposits, but there is growing concern that students make multiple enroll-ment deposits and attend multiple summer orientation programs before they determine which college or university they will attend. As a result, those who run summer orientation programs have become aware that they are still recruiting students. This realization has led to an additional focus on marketing, service, and outreach to students and their families during orientation. In addition, student life units such as housing and campus activities have become increasingly aware that they can help recruit students during the later stages of the recruitment process, particularly when prospective students and their families make campus visits. Tours of residence halls, a meal in an attractive residence hall dining room or food court, or a tour of an active and vibrant college union can have a positive impression on prospective students.

Private institutions usually realize the value of making faculty available to prospective students and their families. During campus visits and events such as off-campus previews, faculty can play an important role. However, these are more recent discoveries for many public colleges and universities. As Litten and Hall (1989) note, both prospective students and their parents regard faculty as a credible source of information. It behooves admissions offices and the faculty who desire better students to become involved in more direct contact with prospective students during the conversion process.

Integrating student affairs, orientation, and academic units is relatively simple at small institutions. It is easier to communicate and to build bridges of cooperation at small colleges and universities. Coordinating the efforts of these offices and departments in large, complex public and private universities can be daunting. A college of engineering may be convinced that it can do a better job than a central admissions office in developing the applicant pool. In such an instance, an individual college or school within a university may create its own undergraduate admissions office. In some instances, prospective students may receive direct mail and telemarketing contacts from two admissions offices at the same institution. The possibility exists that the information might even be conflicting.

Even at smaller schools, many academic programs either fail to understand how they could more strategically use their endowed scholarships, or they simply want to retain full control of their scholarships at all times. In either instance, it may not always be possible to use financial aid to help a campus or for an individual academic unit to use its financial aid in the most effective manner. Yet prospective students and their parents may more actively consider, or eliminate, a college or university on the basis of the overall image that these decentralized, uncoordinated efforts create.

## Tracking the Results

Ongoing tracking and evaluation are difficult but critical elements for effective recruitment. The factors that influence the college enrollment decisions of students are complex. It is not possible through the use of either quantitative or qualitative research and evaluation techniques to identify with confidence the precise set of recruitment activities having the most positive or negative effects on the enrollment decisions of students. However, the new student information systems being installed on many campuses provide ample opportunity to store and retrieve data on the types of contacts the individual institutions have had with prospective students. These data, along with the use of tools like the Admitted Student Questionnaire (contact the College Board for additional information), focus groups, and evaluative surveys used during campus visits, if used repeatedly over time, enable admissions professionals to gauge the relative impact of various recruitment strategies and activities.

"Repeatedly" and "over time" are key phrases. A dramatic decline in applications from a market may be the result of a series of poorly executed previews, or it may be that a major competitor in that region has dramatically increased its financial aid awards. Ongoing tracking and evaluation will reveal whether the decline is just one bad year or the result of fundamental shifts in the region. Monitoring yields at the level of individual geographical markets from prospects to applicants, applicants to admitted students, and admitted students to enrolled students is also important. Shifts in yields can be important indicators. Linking indicators with informed hypotheses regarding trend data can be an effective way to create and find support for new initiatives. For example, the research literature on the effects of campus-based aid suggests that the sooner an institution informs prospective students about the likelihood of receiving financial aid, the greater the impact is on their college choice decision.

With this information in hand, many students admitted to Indiana University for 1999–2000 heard about their campus-based aid two to five months earlier than they did the previous year. As of February 1, 1999, the university was running approximately 30 percent ahead in enrollment deposits. Our working hypothesis is that our efforts to get financial aid information out earlier worked. We do not expect our final yield from admitted to deposited to remain that high, but we are hopeful of an increase in yield of 2 to 5 percent as the result of making campus aid awards earlier. Tracking and evaluating historical yield rates remains an integral part of our efforts.

## The Future

Clearly electronic media will play an increasingly larger role in admissions recruitment. The use of e-mail and the World Wide Web in particular should increase. These two media have the potential for delivering more personalized service, more timely responses, and a lower cost structure. Whether these replace direct mail recruitment remains to be seen.

The use of campus-based financial aid as a recruitment strategy appears likely to continue into the near future. However, the coming of a baby boomlet may reduce the level of competition. Reduced competition could enable campus administrators to see their way clear to reduce the amount of campus-based merit aid over the next decade. This benefit to colleges and universities would be a welcome development for many institutions because increases in campus-based aid have strained the budgets of many colleges and universities.

There will be an increased use of geodemographic tools to refine and segment prospective student markets. In addition, more sophisticated student information systems will facilitate the use of multivariate statistical techniques to assess the efficacy of recruitment strategies. Admissions recruitment will continue down the path toward the use of more social science research methods to help guide activities of admissions offices.

The most important part of successful new student recruitment, however, will remain sound planning and implementation of many of the traditional admissions recruitment strategies.

## References

Abrahamson, T., and Hossler, D. (1990). "Applying Marketing Strategies to Student Recruitment." In D. Hossler and others (eds.), *The Strategic Management of College Enrollments*. San Francisco: Jossey-Bass, 1990.

Anderson, C. "Dear 'Prospective Student': An Analysis of Admissions Materials from Four Universities." *College and University*, 1994, 70(1), 28–26.

Bers, T. "Exploring Institutional Images Through Focus Group Interviews." In R. Lay and J. Endo (eds.), *Designing and Using Market Research*. New Directions for Institutional Research, no. 54. San Francisco: Jossey-Bass, 1987.

Dehne, G. C., Brodigan, D. L., and Topping, P. "Understanding the Marketing of Higher Education." In G. C. Dehne, D. L. Brodigan, and P. Topping (eds.), *Marketing Higher Education: A Handbook for College Administrators*. Washington, D.C.: Consortium for the Advancement of Private Higher Education, 1991.

Gallotti, K. M., and Mark, M. C. "How Do High School Students Structure an Important Life Decision? A Short-Term Longitudinal Study of the College Decision-Making Process." *Research in Higher Education*, 1994, 35 (5), 589–607.

Hossler, D., Braxton, J. M., and Coopersmith, G. "Understanding Student College Choice." In J. C. Smart (ed.), *Higher Education: Handbook of Theory and Research (5)*. New York: Agathon Press, 1989.

Hossler, D., Schmit, J., and Vesper, N. *Going to College: How Social, Economic, and Educational Factors Influence the Decisions Students Make*. Baltimore, Md.: Johns Hopkins University Press, 1998.

Kappler, S. D. "Changing Perspectives: A Side-by-Side Examination of the Differences Between How High School Juniors and Seniors Choose College." Paper presented at the Annual American Marketing Association Meeting on Marketing in Higher Education, San Antonio, Tex., Nov. 1998.

Kotler, P. *Marketing for Nonprofit Organizations*. Englewood Cliffs, N.J.: Prentice-Hall, 1975.

Lewis, G. H., and Morrison, J. *A Longitudinal Study of College Selection*. Technical Report no. 2. Pittsburgh: School of Urban Public Affairs, Carnegie-Mellon University, 1975.

Litten, L. H. "Perspectives on Pricing." In D. Hossler (ed.), *Managing College Enrollments*. New Directions in Higher Education, no. 53. San Francisco: Jossey-Bass, 1986.

Litten, L. H., Sullivan, D. J., and Brodigan, D. L. *Applying Market Research in College Admissions*. New York: College Entrance Examination Board, 1983.

Litten, L. H., and Hall, A. E. "In the Eyes of Our Beholders: Some Evidence on How High School Students and Their Parents View Quality in Colleges." *Journal of Higher Education,* 1989, *60* (2), 302–324.

Paulsen, M. B. *College Choice: Understanding Student Enrollment Behavior.* Washington, D.C.: ERIC Clearinghouse on Higher Education, 1991.

Rothschild, M. "How High School Students Use the Web to Gather Information About Colleges." Paper presented at the Conference on the Net and College Admissions, Chicago, Mar. 1998.

Strauss, D. "The Use of the World Wide Web as a Source of Information During the College Search and Choice Stages of the College Selection Process." Unpublished doctoral dissertation, Ohio State University, 1998.

DON HOSSLER *is professor of educational leadership and policy studies and vice chancellor for enrollment services at Indiana University, Bloomington.*

**3**

*Three retention and enrollment management experts, with more than twenty years' experience working in more than 620 institutions, share their most effective innovations and best practices that have achieved cost-effective results.*

# Strategic Moves for Retention Success

*Randi S. Levitz, Lee Noel, Beth J. Richter*

A revolution appears to be sweeping the campuses of the nation's colleges and universities, and it is based on a simple credo: *The success of an institution and the success of its students are inseparable.* Institutions that take this credo seriously commit the institution—and every individual in it, from the president to faculty members to support staff—to a path of radical and permanent change.

One reason to begin this journey is that many institutions that have already done so have experienced enormous success. A more compelling reason is that institutions that do not may not thrive. There are times when doing nothing is the most dangerous course, and these may well be such times. As budgets tighten, competition for students increases, resources shrink, and regents, legislators, taxpayers, and prospective students and their families take up the cry for institutional accountability, institutions that put students first will succeed, even excel, just as their students will.

The credo also has an important corollary: *Student persistence to the completion of educational goals is a key indicator of student satisfaction and success.* Persistence is an individual performance indicator, and it is measurable. If information on students' goals is collected, preferably at the beginning of each term, then whether an individual student persists to the completion of his or her educational goals can be measured. On the other hand, retention is an institutional performance indicator. In this context the corollary means that student retention is the primary gauge for collectively assessing the success—defined much more broadly than just academic success—of students, and therefore of an institution. Retention, then, is not the primary goal, but it is the best indicator that an institution is meeting its goal of student satisfaction and success. It is a measure of how much student growth and learning takes place, how valued and respected students feel on campus, and how effectively the campus delivers what students expect, need, and want. When these conditions are met, students find a way to stay in school, despite external financial and personal pressures. In sum, retention is a measure of overall "product."

More than a decade ago we coined the phrase *student centeredness* to describe the concept as well as the spirit of campuses that were truly focused on students' needs and, as a result, had very positive retention rates. By putting students squarely at the center of the institution, everyone benefits: students, faculty, staff, and administrators.

In this broader context, retention covers a broad span. If a student's particular educational goals were assessed at the beginning of each term, we could measure persistence—that percentage of students who had met their goals. In the absence of such information, we generally define retention as the percentage of first-time, full-time freshmen who return to the same institution for the second term or second year of study.

Attrition is the flip side of retention, and it has consequences for the student as well as for the image and finances of an institution. An unhappy student who drops out has not only fallen short of meeting a personal goal, but also may negatively influence others about their future choice of that institution. And when a student drops out after the first term or first year, the institution suffers a significant loss of revenue in future years as a result of tuition "lost" to it.

Exhibit 3.1, the Retention Savings Worksheet, provides a way for institutions to calculate the cost of attrition and the "savings" that would occur if the dropout rate were reduced by 10 percent or 20 percent or even 30 percent. The formula does not take into consideration the costs of educating the additional students who persist. The savings is not "net, net." However, the marginal cost of educating each additional unit of enrollment is far less than the average cost of all enrollment units. What is evident in the examples is that even the most modest reduction in attrition rate of 10 percent, meaning a reduction in attrition from 30 percent to 27 percent, would result in savings of hundreds of thousands of dollars even at a very small institution.

## Scope of the Problem

In 1981, Noel and Levitz established a national database at ACT on retention and graduation rates. These data, which provide benchmarks against which individual institutions can measure their own rates, are broken down by type of institution (public or private) and by highest degree offered, as well as by academic selectivity as measured by the average ACT or SAT scores of their entering freshman class. This database has been maintained and updated annually by ACT. The most recent data available appear in Tables 3.1 through 3.4.

As the data indicate in Table 3.1, there is a linear relationship between academic ability and retention. On average, more selective institutions experience lower attrition rates than do less selective institutions. Institutions

## Exhibit 3.1. Retention Savings Worksheet: Calculating the Dollar Value of Reducing Your First-to-Second-Year Dropout Rate

|  | Sample of Public Institution | Sample of Private Institution |
|---|---|---|
| I. Determine the number of students you are losing from first to second year. |  |  |
| A. Enter the number of full-time, first-year students you enrolled ........................................ | 2,000 | 310 |
| B. Enter your first-to-second-year dropout rate (express as a percentage) ....................................... | .30 | .37 |
| C. Total number of students not returning (A × B) .......... | 600 | 115 |
| II. Calculate the dollar value on average of retaining one full-time, first-year dropout to graduation. |  |  |
| A. Enter your tuition (excluding room and board) .......... $ | 3,000 | $ 11,000 |
| B. Enter your average annual per student/district appropriation (if any) .............................. $ | 5,000 | $ |
| C. Calculate your annual gross revenue per student (A + B) ... $ | 8,000 | $ 11,000 |
| D. Enter your average annual tuition discount (unfunded institutional financial aid) .......................... $ | 1,500 | $ 2,970 |
| E. Calculate your average annual net revenue per first-year student (C − D) ................................ $ | 6,500 | $ 8,030 |
| F. Now calculate the value on average of retaining one full-time, first-year dropout to graduation: |  |  |
| 1. Enter your earnings for the freshman year (.25 × E) .... $ | 1,625 | $ 2,007 |
| Assumes that, on average, you will gain some tuition revenue by saving a few freshmen who would have dropped out the first term and who instead continue enrollment (and pay tuition) for second or third term of the freshman year. Estimated tuition saved by additional term(s) of enrollment during freshman year = 25 percent. |  |  |
| 2. Enter your earnings for the sophomore year (.90 × E) .. $ | 5,850 | $ 7,227 |
| Assumes 90 percent of the saved freshmen* will complete the sophomore year. |  |  |
| Two-year institutions, skip to G; four-year institutions, please continue. |  |  |
| 3. Enter your earnings for the junior year (.80 × E) ....... $ | 5,200 | $ 6,424 |
| Assumes 80 percent of the saved freshmen will complete the junior year. |  |  |
| 4. Enter your earnings for the senior year (.70 × E) ...... $ | 4,550 | $ 5,621 |
| Assumes 70 percent of the saved freshmen will complete the senior year. |  |  |
| G. Total net revenue on average gained by retaining one full-time, first-year dropout to graduation: (Two-year institutions, 1 + 2; four-year institutions, 1 + 2 + 3 + 4) ..................................... $ | 17,225 | $ 21,279 |
| III. Calculate the dollar value of reducing your first-to-second-year dropout rate. |  |  |
| A. Enter the number of first-year students you are losing to attrition (I.C) | 600 | 115 |
| B. Enter the total net revenue gained by retaining one such student to graduation (II.G) | $ 17,225 | $ 21,279 |
| C. Total dollar value of reducing your first-to-second-year dropout rate by 10, 20, or 30 percent: |  |  |
| ➤ 10 percent reduction [(.10 × A) × B] .................. | $1,033,500 | $ 244,709 |
| ➤ 20 percent reduction [(.20 × A) × B] .................. | $2,067,000 | $ 489,417 |
| ➤ 30 percent reduction [(.30 × A) × B] .................. | $3,100,500 | $ 734,126 |

*Saved freshmen refers only to that group of freshmen who were *prevented* from dropping out as freshmen.

**Table 3.1. Freshman-to-Sophomore-Year Dropout Rate by Admissions Selectivity for Institutions Reporting Cut-Off Scores**

| | | *Typical Test Scores* | | |
| --- | --- | --- | --- | --- |
| *Selectivity Level* | *ACT* | *SAT* | *Number* | *Mean Percentage* |
| Highly selective | ≥27.0 | ≥1220 | 120 | 8.4 |
| Selective | 22.0–26.9 | 1030–1219 | 414 | 18.3 |
| Traditional | 20.0–21.9 | 950–1029 | 696 | 27.1 |
| Liberal | 18.0–19.9 | 870–949 | 393 | 35.2 |
| Open | <18.0 | <870 | 892 | 45.7 |
| Number of institutions | | | 2,515 | |

*Source:* Compiled from ACT Institutional Data File, 1999. (©1999. The American College Testing Program. All Rights Reserved.)

**Table 3.2. Freshman-to-Sophomore-Year Dropout Rate by Type of Institution**

| *Degree Level/Control* | *Number* | *Mean Percentage* |
| --- | --- | --- |
| Two-year public | 752 | 47.5 |
| Two-year private | 141 | 30.1 |
| BA/BS public | 66 | 33.3 |
| BA/BS private | 481 | 28.6 |
| MA/first professional, public | 231 | 30.5 |
| MA/first professional, private | 483 | 24.0 |
| PhD public | 198 | 23.5 |
| PhD private | 162 | 16.4 |
| Number of institutions | 2,514 | 32.6 |

*Source:* Compiled from ACT Institutional Data File, 1999. (©1999. The American College Testing Program. All Rights Reserved.)

that report the highest average ACT and SAT scores have an average first-to-second-year dropout rate of less than 9 percent, with open-door institutions having a first-to-second-year dropout rate that is more than five times higher, or 46 percent. This is not to suggest that institutions should make qualitative judgments on the basis of selectivity. Selectivity may be related to the institution's mission, which may include an emphasis on access. Some of the most exciting and student-centered education can be found at open-door institutions as well as those serving average or below-average ACT/SAT-scoring incoming students. Moreover, there is great variation among similar types of institutions even when they admit students with similar levels of academic ability.

### Table 3.3. Freshman-to-Sophomore-Year Dropout Rates by Type and Selectivity of Institution, Public

| Self-Reported Admissions Selectivity | | Associate | BA | MA | PhD |
|---|---|---|---|---|---|
| Highly selective | Mean percentage = | NA | 11.8 | 10.3 | 9.0 |
| ACT ≥27.0 | Number = | | 4 | 4 | 19 |
| SAT ≥1220 | Standard deviation = | | 4.8 | 3.4 | 4.7 |
| Selective | Mean percentage = | NA | 20.6 | 21.4 | 19.5 |
| ACT 22.0–26.9 | Number = | 1 | 5 | 43 | 76 |
| SAT 1030–1219 | Standard deviation = | | 6.8 | 6.3 | 7.4 |
| Traditional | Mean percentage = | 27.7 | 30.3 | 29.1 | 27.6 |
| ACT 20.0–21.9 | Number = | 16 | 24 | 109 | 76 |
| SAT 950–1029 | Standard deviation = | 9.9 | 9.1 | 7.6 | 6.2 |
| Liberal | Mean percentage = | 45.6 | 34.4 | 34.1 | 32.4 |
| ACT 18.0–19.9 | Number = | 45 | 13 | 35 | 20 |
| SAT 870–949 | Standard deviation = | 12.9 | 10.2 | 9.1 | 9.6 |
| Open | Mean percentage = | 48.1 | 43.9 | 43.0 | 35.0 |
| ACT <18 | Number = | 691 | 20 | 40 | 7 |
| SAT <870 | Standard deviation = | 15.1 | 11.9 | 12.4 | 3.7 |
| Number of Institutions | | 752 | 66 | 231 | 198 |

*Source:* Compiled from ACT Institutional Data File, 1999. (©1999. The American College Testing Program. All Rights Reserved.)

Table 3.2 displays dropout rates by type of institution; in each case, dropout rates are lower among private institutions than they are for public institutions. Table 3.3 displays dropout rates for public institutions by type *and* admissions selectivity, and Table 3.4 displays similar data for private institutions. These data provide good benchmarks against which institutions can measure their standing.

Probably the most interesting aspect of the data is the variation in dropout rates at similar types of institutions. For example in Table 3.3, the 109 master's-degree-granting public institutions whose entering freshmen average ACT scores of 20.0 to 21.9 or SAT scores of 950 to 1029 have an average dropout rate of 29.1, with a standard deviation of 7.6. If these institutions were normally distributed, the dropout rates for 68 percent of the institutions in this group (plus or minus one standard deviation) ranged from a low of 21.5 percent to a high of 36.7 percent.

In Table 3.4, the 241 master's-degree-granting private institutions whose entering freshmen average ACT scores of 20.0 to 21.9 or SAT scores of 950 to 1029 have an average dropout rate of 25.7 percent, with a standard deviation of 8.9. If these institutions were normally distributed, the

**Table 3.4.  Freshman-to-Sophomore-Year Dropout Rates by Type and Selectivity of Institution, Private**

| Self-Reported Admissions Selectivity | | Associate | BA | MA | PhD |
|---|---|---|---|---|---|
| Highly selective | Mean percentage = | NA | 7.7 | 9.0 | 7.4 |
| ACT ≥27.0 | Number = | 1 | 27 | 23 | 42 |
| SAT ≥1220 | Standard deviation = | | 5.9 | 4.0 | 4.8 |
| Selective | Mean percentage = | 7.3 | 18.4 | 18.5 | 14.6 |
| ACT 22.0–26.9 | Number = | 3 | 100 | 127 | 59 |
| SAT 1030–1219 | Standard deviation = | 6.4 | 7.1 | 7.9 | 5.3 |
| Traditional | Mean percentage = | 22.8 | 29.2 | 25.7 | 22.8 |
| ACT 20.0–21.9 | Number = | 25 | 155 | 241 | 50 |
| SAT 950–1029 | Standard deviation = | 17.1 | 11.0 | 8.9 | 7.8 |
| Liberal | Mean percentage = | 32.1 | 36.6 | 30.1 | 34.6 |
| ACT 18.0–19.9 | Number = | 72 | 131 | 68 | 9 |
| SAT 870–949 | Standard deviation = | 16.1 | 14.1 | 10.6 | 12.7 |
| Open | Mean percentage = | 35.8 | 35.8 | 32.2 | 17.0 |
| ACT <18 | Number = | 41 | 67 | 24 | 2 |
| SAT <870 | Standard deviation = | 20.1 | 19.2 | 17.1 | 17.0 |
| Number of Institutions | | 141 | 481 | 483 | 162 |

*Source:* Compiled from ACT Institutional Data File, 1999. (©1999. The American College Testing Program. All Rights Reserved.)

dropout rates for 68 percent of the private institutions in this group (plus or minus one standard deviation) ranged from a low of 16.8 percent to a high of 34.6 percent. The highest standard deviations were observed in the open-door public and private associate-degree-granting institutions shown in Tables 3.3 and 3.4.

There is a reason for such wide variation within these groups of similar institutions. Institutions *can* control their dropout rates to a great extent based on the energy and effort that is put into getting students started right on the path into and through the first year of college. Institutions that provide adequate personal and programmatic support through orientation, advising, and careful attention to introductory course experiences realize lower dropout rates. This was first noted by Aubrey Forrest (1982); we too have made hundreds of similar observations on the college and university campuses we have visited.

## Why Focus on the First Year?

The first-to-second-year attrition rate is perhaps the most important determiner of an institution's graduation rate. We have observed that attrition rates are halved each subsequent year after the first year. For example, if an institution has a first-to-second year attrition rate of 30 percent for an entering freshman class, attrition after the second year is commonly half that (15 percent); it is half that again (8 percent) after the third year, 4 percent after the fourth, and 2 percent during the fifth year. The graduation rate can then be calculated by adding up these rates, and subtracting the sum from 100 percent. For this example, the five-year graduation rate would be calculated as follows: 100 percent − (30 + 15 + 8 + 4 + 2) = 41 percent. Given this finding, it is clear that the most efficient way to boost graduation rates is to reduce the first-to-second-year attrition rate. Tables 3.5 and 3.6 depict graduation rates by institutional type and selectivity of entering freshman classes. The rates are calculated within three years for students pursuing associate degrees and within five years for students pursuing baccalaureate degrees.

As is true nationwide, freshmen enter with some anxiety or apprehension about beginning a new educational venture. Some of these students also bring complex educational and personal issues that dictate the need for even more comprehensive and individualized support services than institutions are currently set up to provide. And further, our recent research suggests that affective variables (such as study habits, academic confidence, desire to finish college, attitude toward educators, self-reliance, family emotional support, and openness) contribute much more to attrition than was ever thought to be the case.

Well-meaning teachers and advisers typically ask freshmen how they are doing at some point during the critical first term of the first year. And typically the answer is, "Fine," regardless of the characteristics of the student, institution, or region of the country. Yet we have found that students are not so fine after all. Listed below are some comments freshmen have made to us this past year:

- I don't know what to say to my adviser.
- I'm scared.
- I feel like giving up.
- I feel lost and confused.
- I don't know where to go.
- I don't know what I'm supposed to do.
- I don't understand what my teacher is saying.
- I don't understand what my teacher wants.
- I can't juggle kids and school and home.
- I didn't think college would be like this.
- I start something, and then I start something else.
- I could never go see my teacher after class; only the smartest students go.
- I don't know how to make new friends.
- I'll never get good grades here.
- I wasn't cut out to be a student twenty years ago, and I'm not student material now either.

**Table 3.5. National Graduation Rates by Type of Institution and Level of Selectivity, Public**

| *Self-Reported Admissions Selectivity* | | *Associate* | *BA* | *MA* | *PhD* |
|---|---|---|---|---|---|
| Highly selective | Mean percentage = | | 70.0 | 67.3 | 72.7 |
| ACT ≥27.0 | Number = | NA | 4 | 4 | 20 |
| SAT ≥1220 | Standard deviation = | | 15.9 | 12.4 | 12.2 |
| Selective | Mean percentage = | NA | 62.2 | 43.3 | 50.8 |
| ACT 22.0–26.9 | Number = | 1 | 5 | 41 | 74 |
| SAT 1030–1219 | Standard deviation = | | 17.3 | 19.0 | 16.6 |
| Traditional | Mean percentage = | 33.1 | 40.8 | 40.2 | 37.3 |
| ACT 20.0–21.9 | Number = | 16 | 22 | 102 | 75 |
| SAT 950–1029 | Standard deviation = | 15.7 | 18.2 | 14.0 | 12.7 |
| Liberal | Mean percentage = | 42.8 | 42.3 | 30.3 | 34.4 |
| ACT 18.0–19.9 | Number = | 45 | 11 | 33 | 18 |
| SAT 870–949 | Standard deviation = | 22.5 | 20.7 | 13.6 | 20.4 |
| Open | Mean percentage = | 32.5 | 30.9 | 31.0 | 30.3 |
| ACT <18 | Number = | 720 | 12 | 23 | 6 |
| SAT <870 | Standard deviation = | 19.8 | 13.8 | 14.6 | 14.7 |
| Number of Institutions | | 771 | 54 | 203 | 190 |

*Note:* Graduation in three years for associate degree; five years for BA or BS

*Source:* Compiled from ACT Institutional Data File, 1999. (©1999. The American College Testing Program. All Rights Reserved.)

- I don't know what to do first.
- I don't think my teachers like me.
- I feel really different than the other students here.

Those of us in academia tend to assume that virtually all students are ready to succeed and persist. But in reality, we have probably overrated students' abilities in the following areas:

- Learning the norms of campus culture
- Finding a niche
- Putting down roots
- Transferring successful behaviors from other settings
- Developing focus
- Resisting peer pressures
- Compartmentalizing family and work pressures
- Exhibiting classroom habits of successful students
- Building relationships with teachers
- Asking for help

**Table 3.6. National Graduation Rates by Type of Institution and Level of Selectivity, Private**

| Self-Reported Admissions Selectivity | | Associate | BA | MA | PhD |
|---|---|---|---|---|---|
| Highly selective | Mean percentage = | | 82.9 | 75.7 | 81.6 |
| ACT ≥27.0 | Number = | NA | 29 | 23 | 41 |
| SAT ≥1220 | Standard deviation = | | 10.5 | 10.2 | 12.0 |
| Selective | Mean percentage = | 75.0 | 65.2 | 61.8 | 65.5 |
| ACT 22.0–26.9 | Number = | 4 | 95 | 120 | 60 |
| SAT 1030–1219 | Standard deviation = | 4.1 | 11.1 | 12.0 | 12.1 |
| Traditional | Mean percentage = | 66.6 | 52.4 | 52.8 | 50.2 |
| ACT 20.0–21.9 | Number = | 23 | 139 | 218 | 49 |
| SAT 950–1029 | Standard deviation = | 19.3 | 14.3 | 13.7 | 16.3 |
| Liberal | Mean percentage = | 61.5 | 42.1 | 43.1 | 48.2 |
| ACT 18.0–19.9 | Number = | 77 | 93 | 57 | 9 |
| SAT 870–949 | Standard deviation = | 20.4 | 17.8 | 17.6 | 23.3 |
| Open | Mean percentage = | 55.1 | 39.2 | 43.6 | 31.0 |
| ACT <18 | Number = | 45 | 43 | 19 | 2 |
| SAT <870 | Standard deviation = | 24.8 | 18.8 | 22.8 | 15.6 |
| Number of Institutions | | 149 | 398 | 437 | 161 |

Note: Graduation in three years for associate degree; five years for BA or BS

Source: Compiled from ACT Institutional Data File, 1999. (©1999. The American College Testing Program. All Rights Reserved.)

Getting students started right on the path through the institution to graduation begins with anticipating and meeting their transition and adjustment needs when they enter. Freshmen need a prevention plan. Intrusive, proactive strategies must be used to reach freshmen before the students have an opportunity to experience feelings of failure, disappointment, and confusion.

Withdrawing-student surveys always list money, time, and personal reasons in answer to the question of why they are leaving. Yet our experience indicates that these are but the surface reasons. Levitz and Hovland (1998) have listed five categories of issues facing students that ultimately have an impact on the decision to drop out:

Personal: Lost, stressed, closed to new ideas and experiences, undisciplined, unmotivated, insecure, uninformed, unrealistic expectations, student-institution mismatch

Social: Alienation and social isolation, subject to negative peer pressure, uninvolved in college activities, little involvement with faculty members or advisers

Academic: Underprepared, underchallenged, poor study habits, does not see value in assignments and courses, low academic performance, part-time course load, lack of educational and career goals, feedback that is too little too late

Life issues: Insecurity about financial circumstances, job and school time conflicts, home and family difficulties, personal problems, health problems, college not necessary to meet career goals

Institutional issues: Experience the run-around; experience operational problems (for example, in billing and scheduling); experience negative attitudes in classrooms, advising centers, administrative offices; experience poor or indifferent teaching; encounter instructional equipment or technology that is out of date; academic program not available

Students may well have the potential to be highly motivated, independent student-scholars. However, hundreds of anecdotal reports from faculty and staff members across the nation indicate that a majority of the students today lack the level of independence, skill, and savvy of students in years past. This evidence suggests that a primary goal for an institution should be to move students from low or no levels of commitment (intellectual, emotional, social) to the point where they become independent learners. But the assumption that most students come in as truly independent learners is far too common and thereby inhibits the active, even intrusive programming needed to reduce dropout rates. Institutions must find ways to partner with students to cause the kind of transformational development to take place that will move those who are prone to drop out into the persisters' camp.

## A Step-by-Step Approach to Retention Results

Virtually every program, person, and procedure on a campus has the potential to have an impact on students, and therefore on retention. But there are conflicting axioms: when everyone is responsible, no one is responsible; when no one is responsible, nothing gets done. And the job is simply too big for one person or one office to handle. Yet there is a step-by-step path out of this conundrum that several hundred institutions have followed.

For maximum impact, retention improvement efforts can proceed on two planes: an immediate individualized approach that can be quickly implemented and a longer-term effort that will lead to substantive, long-lasting changes in institutional culture.

**Immediate Individualized Approach.** While a task force is organizing and broader retention issues are being discussed and researched, campuses have begun to take concrete steps to jump-start their retention improvement effort. The successful implementation of an individualized student approach delivers substantial results almost immediately because it is based on the concept that attitude and motivation are better predictors of who stays and who leaves than are traditional cognitive measures. By building on this research-based insight, an institution can identify specific dropout prevention plans for incoming students and, importantly, leverage time. Very few institutions today have unlimited resources for helping students get a good start in college. Therefore, an institution that is able to direct resources of time, energy, and money toward students who are most likely to be prone to drop out, who most need and want help, *and* who are willing to be helped has truly leveraged its resources.

Nearly five hundred colleges and universities are using the Retention Management System (RMS) to identify the extent to which their incoming freshmen are prone to drop out, and if so, what type of intervention will be needed and whether the student will be receptive to that intervention. These schools report that this system enables them to fold a triage approach into their retention practice. The RMS uses scales to identify degrees of dropout-proneness and receptivity to help. The school can therefore reach out immediately to the most dropout-prone students who are likely to be responsive. As resources are available, they then focus attention on subsequent levels of dropout-prone students.

Colleges and universities report increased retention success from working with students who did not appear to be at risk because their traditional cognitive performance (high school grades and test scores) was adequate, while the RMS uncovered attitudinal and motivational issues that may have led to dropout-prone behavior if left unchecked.

**Longer-Term Approach.** Maximum improvement in retention performance requires implementation of programs that lead to long-lasting campus culture changes. The best retention programs have the following characteristics:

Highly structured. Student success is not left to chance. The institution views itself as responsible for creating a success structure rather than merely retaining a reactive sink-or-swim philosophy.

Extended, intensive contact with students who are most likely to drop out. For these students retention is a one-on-one activity, and results are predicated on a personal relationship. In order to get retention power out of academic advising, advisors need to understand the affective needs and motivation levels of the individual student and time to establish a relationship.

Interlocks with other programs and services. For example, academic advising should be woven into the fabric of a required freshman success course.

A strategy of engagement. Students are brought into situations in which the risk of participation is reduced. That is, the faculty or staff member takes the initiative to reach out to bring the student into the fold rather than assume a passive stance that offers students the opportunity to participate.

Qualified staff. Qualifications go far beyond credentials for a position to include attitude and ability to build relationships. There is increased emphasis on the importance of a student-centered environment everywhere on campus. This message is communicated clearly at point of hire and is reinforced through follow-up development and training activities.

A critical role for faculty members. It is extraordinarily important to have rewards and recognition in place for excellent teaching. A single "Teacher of the Year" award is too unattainable and further sends a message that great teaching, especially in the freshman classroom, is nice but not necessary. Ultimately the tenure and promotion criteria established and adhered to are the determiners of whether intense energy is devoted to becoming a great teacher in the freshman classroom. Until that happens, providing "great teaching" awards, with modest monetary awards, for 10 to 20 percent of the teaching faculty will begin to capture the attention of faculty members, causing some to adjust their classroom behavior.

A focus on the affective as well as cognitive needs of students. Far too little attention is usually paid to how students are coping: whether they are getting connected to the new environment or feeling lost, confused, or overwhelmed. Attention to the individual needs of students can set them on a course for success.

Improving retention means change, which never comes easily. Some will protest, "We've always done it this way!" or "We don't have the money [or time]." Following are some tips for getting started with the change process.

*Establish a retention task force, even if the campus already has a retention coordinator.* Commitment to the cause is most readily gained when people have a chance to participate. Because so much institutional power rests with the faculty, it is critical that task force membership be heavily weighted toward the academic side of the campus—while taking great care to reinforce the valuable role played by student affairs staff.

The initial task force members should be those who see students as individuals and have a passion for watching them grow, develop, and succeed. It is likely to be counterproductive to include cynics or those who believe in the sink-or-swim approach. Such members tend to extend the debate and needlessly delay the development and implementation of action plans.

If a retention task force has been in existence for some time and results have not been forthcoming, a separate task force on student success should be established.

*Carefully select the person to head the retention task force.* This person, so central to the task force's success, needs the vision and the courage to activate it. It is essential that the task force have the weight of the office of the president behind it. The retention task force puts forth the recommended platform, and the president backs it with necessary resources, clearing institutional obstacles that may arise. (On a large university campus, this effort might initially be more effective if undertaken within an individual school, for example, the College of Arts and Sciences, rather than throughout the university.)

*Make sure the task force spends a minimum amount of time studying the issue despite the natural tendency to want to explore every potential alternative.* The majority of the task force's time should be spent deciding on a plan of action that fits the campus. Before that can take place, the affected parties and the institution need to establish priorities for retention improvement effort. The most effective way of determining those priorities is to assess what is most important to students and how satisfied they are with each of these areas. A student satisfaction inventory is an ideal tool to identify performance gaps—areas to attack first. On the other hand, there should not be too many initiatives. Most campuses that establish seventeen or more initiatives may feel as if they have a comprehensive, campuswide plan, but they lack the focus and intensity needed to get results. The task force should start with two to four priorities that are most critical and then mobilize the energy and resources necessary to make them happen.

*Establish a readiness to accept change across the campus by promoting a widespread understanding of what retention is and what it is not.* Data can be drawn on to debunk the myths (such as that dropouts are flunkouts) and clearly identify the potential benefits for all parties if retention improves. Forums for discussing ideas for good retention practice and the planks of the retention platform will be fleshed out in this process. These efforts will minimize the extent to which people on campus feel compelled to protect their turf, and the natural resistance to change will be somewhat reduced by helping people across campus understand the benefits of improved retention. (This may need to be done within schools in a university.)

*Go for big gains.* Small pilot programs, programs that are designed solely for academically high-risk students, and minor revisions in existing orientation or advising programs seldom get broad enough or impressive enough results to convince the skeptics (or even supporters) that the program has high gain potential.

Pilot programs involve too few students to reduce the dropout rate. Further, their design often is based on students who volunteer, and are therefore less likely to drop out anyway, or students who are so at risk that the results cannot be generalized. Pilot programs are useful in perfecting a program's design and delivery strategies. After this initial test stage, it is tempting to launch increasingly larger pilot projects, but in our experience, these efforts usually run out of steam before producing exciting results. It is far more effective to launch a new program, such as a student success course, with an entire incoming freshman class, and then conduct a retrospective comparison of retention rates with a previous entering class, controlling for academic ability and achievement as measured by ACT or SAT scores.

*Celebrate successes!* There is nothing like a party atmosphere to reenergize people who feel burned out. Some of the most creative, low-cost rewards we have seen for members of the retention task force include highly prized campus parking spots reserved for a month, tickets to popular campus athletic events, certificates for dinner in a local restaurant, and movie passes or tickets to a campus concert or play, as well as the ever-popular dinner at the president's house, cooked by the president. These work equally well for stellar advisers, counselors, and faculty members who make a tremendous difference in the lives of students.

Even a small monetary incentive pays big dividends. Modest stipends when combined with recognition do wonders to motivate people to the next level of performance.

**Setting the Retention Agenda.** In our experience, campuses attempt to work on too broad a retention agenda, which has a number of negative consequences. Not only are there no successes to celebrate, but everyone feels defeated. Prioritizing a retention improvement agenda is critical. To date nearly nine hundred institutions have used the Student Satisfaction Inventory (SSI) to establish retention priorities. The SSI determines levels of importance that students assign to various aspects of the institution as well as their level of satisfaction with each of these. This two-dimensional approach allows institutions to calculate "performance gaps"—by subtracting satisfaction scores from importance scores—that permit the identification of student concerns that ultimately affect student success and persistence. By illuminating which aspects of the campus experience students consider most and least important, along with how satisfied students are in these areas, the SSI provides a vehicle for institutions to set priorities that are closely aligned with those of their students.

Tables 3.7 through 3.9 present the most recent National Student Satisfaction Report by institutional type. Each item on the SSI is expressed as a statement of expectation, and students are asked to rate the level of importance they assign to the expectation as well as their level of satisfaction that the expectation is being met by their campus. The rating scale ranges from 1 (low) to 7 (high). The performance gap is calculated by subtracting the Satisfaction ranking from the Importance ranking. When these data are collected on individual campuses, the size of the performance gap in relation to an item's importance helps determine whether the item should be addressed as part of a retention effort. Nearly all institutions also compare their students' level of satisfaction with each aspect with those of students in similar types of institutions. This gives them a general measure of how their performance measures up to performance in other similar type institutions.

Table 3.7 contains data from 158,133 students in four-year public institutions and displays the top twenty-five items (out of seventy-three) in order of importance. The first six items given the highest importance ranking by students focus on academic-related issues: content of courses, quality of instruction, the extent to which teachers and advisers are knowledgeable, and the ability to register for needed classes.

**Table 3.7. Student Satisfaction Rating, Four-Year
Public Colleges and Universities**

| Item | Importance | Satisfaction | Performance Gap |
|---|---|---|---|
| The content of the courses within my major is valuable. | 6.56 | 5.27 | 1.29 |
| The instruction in my major field is excellent. | 6.54 | 5.22 | 1.32 |
| I am able to register for classes I need with few conflicts. | 6.54 | 4.55 | 1.99 |
| Nearly all of the faculty are knowledgeable in their field. | 6.51 | 5.52 | 0.99 |
| My academic advisor is knowledgeable about requirements in my major. | 6.50 | 5.31 | 1.19 |
| The quality of instruction I receive in most of my classes is excellent. | 6.49 | 5.10 | 1.39 |
| The campus is safe and secure for all students. | 6.45 | 5.16 | 1.29 |
| My academic advisor is approachable. | 6.42 | 5.21 | 1.21 |
| There is a good variety of courses provided on this campus. | 6.42 | 5.22 | 1.20 |
| Tuition paid is a worthwhile investment. | 6.41 | 4.93 | 1.48 |
| Faculty are fair and unbiased in their treatment of individual students. | 6.38 | 4.85 | 1.53 |
| Major requirements are clear and reasonable. | 6.37 | 5.10 | 1.27 |
| Faculty are usually available after class and during office hours. | 6.35 | 5.35 | 1.00 |
| I am able to experience intellectual growth here. | 6.33 | 5.34 | 0.99 |
| Computer labs are adequate and accessible. | 6.30 | 4.77 | 1.53 |
| Library resources and services are adequate. | 6.27 | 5.01 | 1.26 |
| There is a commitment to academic excellence on this campus. | 6.26 | 5.05 | 1.21 |
| The campus staff are caring and helpful. | 6.24 | 4.91 | 1.33 |
| My academic advisor is concerned about my success as an individual. | 6.24 | 4.90 | 1.34 |
| Adequate financial aid is available for most students. | 6.23 | 4.34 | 1.89 |
| Faculty provide timely feedback about student progress in a course. | 6.22 | 4.73 | 1.49 |
| Parking lots are well-lighted and secure. | 6.21 | 4.60 | 1.61 |
| It is an enjoyable experience to be a student on this campus. | 6.21 | 5.05 | 1.16 |
| The amount of student parking space on campus is adequate. | 6.20 | 2.91 | 3.29 |
| This institution shows concern for students as individuals. | 6.20 | 4.63 | 1.57 |

*National Student Satisfaction Report.* Iowa City, Iowa: Noel-Levitz, 1999. Available online at http://www.noellevitz.com/res/research/99studsatrep.pdf

*Note:* The scale ranges from 1 (not important/not satisfied at all) to 7 (very important/very satisfied).

## Table 3.8. Student Satisfaction Rating, Four-Year Private Colleges and Universities

| Item | Importance | Satisfaction | Performance Gap |
|---|---|---|---|
| The content of the courses within my major is valuable. | 6.62 | 5.50 | 1.12 |
| The instruction in my major field is excellent. | 6.60 | 5.45 | 1.15 |
| Nearly all of the faculty are knowledgeable in their field. | 6.55 | 5.74 | 0.81 |
| The quality of instruction I receive in most of my classes is excellent. | 6.54 | 5.43 | 1.11 |
| I am able to register for classes I need with few conflicts. | 6.49 | 4.93 | 1.56 |
| My academic advisor is knowledgeable about requirements in my major. | 6.47 | 5.49 | 0.98 |
| Tuition paid is a worthwhile investment. | 6.47 | 4.75 | 1.72 |
| The campus is safe and secure for all students. | 6.44 | 5.45 | 0.99 |
| I am able to experience intellectual growth here. | 6.43 | 5.52 | 0.91 |
| Faculty are fair and unbiased in their treatment of individual students. | 6.41 | 5.08 | 1.33 |
| There is a good variety of courses provided on this campus. | 6.41 | 5.10 | 1.31 |
| My academic advisor is approachable. | 6.40 | 5.53 | 0.87 |
| Adequate financial aid is available for most students. | 6.40 | 4.67 | 1.73 |
| There is a commitment to academic excellence on this campus. | 6.37 | 5.43 | 1.24 |
| Major requirements are clear and reasonable. | 6.37 | 5.38 | 0.99 |
| It is an enjoyable experience to be a student on this campus. | 6.35 | 5.26 | 1.09 |
| Faculty are usually available after class and during office hours. | 6.35 | 5.56 | 0.79 |
| The campus staff are caring and helpful. | 6.34 | 5.40 | 0.94 |
| This institution shows concern for students as individuals. | 6.34 | 5.22 | 1.12 |
| Computer labs are adequate and accessible. | 6.31 | 4.80 | 1.51 |
| My academic advisor is concerned about my success as an individual. | 6.27 | 5.29 | 0.98 |
| Students are made to feel welcome on this campus. | 6.27 | 5.39 | 0.88 |
| Faculty care about me as an individual. | 6.25 | 5.35 | 0.90 |
| Library resources and services are adequate. | 6.25 | 4.73 | 1.52 |
| Faculty provide timely feedback about student progress in a course. | 6.24 | 5.01 | 1.23 |

*National Student Satisfaction Report.* Iowa City, Iowa: Noel-Levitz, 1999.

*Notes:* The scale ranges from 1 (not important/not satisfied at all) to 7 (very important/very satisfied).

Table 3.8 contains data from 261,934 students and displays the top 25 items (out of 73) in order of importance.

## Table 3.9. Student Satisfaction Rating, Community, Junior, and Technical Colleges

| Item | Importance | Satisfaction | Performance Gap |
|---|---|---|---|
| The quality of instruction I receive in most of my classes is excellent. | 6.48 | 5.53 | 0.95 |
| Classes are scheduled at times that are convenient for me. | 6.45 | 5.33 | 1.12 |
| I am able to register for classes I need with few conflicts. | 6.33 | 5.25 | 1.08 |
| Nearly all of the faculty are knowledgeable in their fields. | 6.33 | 5.60 | 0.73 |
| There is a good variety of courses provided on this campus. | 6.29 | 5.38 | 0.91 |
| I am able to experience intellectual growth here. | 6.28 | 5.54 | 0.74 |
| The campus is safe and secure for all students. | 6.27 | 5.33 | 0.94 |
| My academic advisor is knowledgeable about my program requirements. | 6.26 | 5.28 | 0.98 |
| Faculty are fair and unbiased in their treatment of individual students. | 6.24 | 5.18 | 1.06 |
| Program requirements are clear and reasonable. | 6.24 | 5.41 | 0.83 |
| This school does whatever it can to help me reach my educational goals. | 6.21 | 5.07 | 1.14 |
| Faculty are usually available after class and during office hours. | 6.21 | 5.50 | 0.71 |
| My academic advisor is approachable. | 6.19 | 5.34 | 0.85 |
| Library resources and services are adequate. | 6.19 | 5.19 | 1.00 |
| Adequate financial aid is available for most students. | 6.17 | 4.96 | 1.21 |
| Computer labs are adequate and accessible. | 6.16 | 5.11 | 1.05 |
| Students are notified early in the term if they are doing poorly in a class. | 6.16 | 4.86 | 1.30 |
| Parking lots are well-lighted and secure. | 6.15 | 4.84 | 1.31 |
| Policies and procedures regarding registration and course selection are clear and well-publicized. | 6.15 | 5.30 | 0.85 |
| The amount of student parking space on campus is adequate. | 6.15 | 4.24 | 1.91 |
| The equipment in the lab facilities is kept up to date. | 6.14 | 5.09 | 1.05 |
| The personnel involved in registration are helpful. | 6.13 | 5.29 | 0.84 |
| The college shows concern for students as individuals. | 6.13 | 4.98 | 1.15 |
| Faculty provide timely feedback about student progress in a course. | 6.13 | 5.17 | 0.96 |
| There are convenient ways of paying my school bill. | 6.13 | 5.17 | 0.96 |

*National Student Satisfaction Report.* Iowa City, Iowa: Noel-Levitz, 1999.

*Notes:* The scale ranges from 1 (not important/not satisfied at all) to 7 (very important/very satisfied).

Table 3.9 contains data from 181,278 students and displays the top 25 items (out of 73) in order of importance.

These data and their importance rankings are critical in prioritizing areas for improvement on a given campus. Consider, for example, the amount of available student parking, which is often a topic of conversation and complaint on campus, yet it is listed twenty-fourth in importance. Students are not likely to feel satisfied with parking unless they are practically guaranteed a parking space directly in front of their class building. Therefore, addressing the parking issue would not be as critical a retention agenda item as making certain that students are able to register for needed classes. That is the third item listed in importance and has a performance gap of 1.99. Increasing student satisfaction in this area and thereby closing this perceived performance gap will pay retention dividends.

Expectations are critical: they serve as the point from which students make qualitative judgments about an institution. Measuring the level of student satisfaction outside the context of what is expected (or the level of importance) is incomplete, and perhaps even dangerous. Such practice frequently leads to doing things right rather than doing the right things.

## Overcoming the "No-Money Syndrome"

Institutions that elect to invest additional dollars into bringing their recruitment operations to state-of-the-art levels get state-of-the-art results quickly. Yet even in those institutions, it seems that there are never extra dollars available to breathe more life into retention-related people and programming.

Too often, reducing the dropout rate is not recognized as one of the most effective ways to add full-time equivalents, thereby broadening an institution's revenue base. Our research shows that by reducing the number of freshmen dropouts by a single student, a four-year institution will, on average, "save" $15,000 to $25,000 in gross revenue over four to five years. (See Exhibit 3.1.) Investing in retention programming is good business. Few, if any, other institutional investments will yield such a high return.

Increased retention results in substantial savings for even the smallest of institutions, and millions of dollars to the largest.

Beyond the budgetary impact of improved retention, increases in student satisfaction are worth their weight in gold as current students talk with prospective students in their families, schools, workplaces, and home towns. Student success and institutional success are truly inseparable.

## References

Forrest, A. *Increasing Student Competence and Persistence.* Iowa City, Iowa: ACT National Center for the Advancement of Educational Practices, 1982.
Levitz, R., and Hovland, M. "Dropout Prone Students." In Noel, L., and Levitz, R. (eds.), *Power Strategies for Recruitment and Retention Workshop Notebook.* Iowa City: Noel-Levitz, 1998.

*RANDI S. LEVITZ is senior executive and cofounder of Noel-Levitz and is nationally recognized for her pathbreaking work in retention and enrollment management.*

*LEE NOEL is senior executive and cofounder of Noel-Levitz, who has pioneered retention programs and is nationally recognized for providing comprehensive enrollment management counsel.*

*BETH J. RICHTER is program consultant at Noel-Levitz who specializes in intervention programs designed to increase student success and retention.*

4

*With funding from the Pew Charitable Trusts, a group of ten historically black colleges and universities developed databases and programs that resulted in increased retention and progression. Now these institutions are collaborating and are ready to offer a series of useful lessons for others wishing to make a difference for academically at-risk students.*

# Student Retention and Progression: A Special Challenge for Private Historically Black Colleges and Universities

*Michael T. Nettles, Ursula Wagener, Catherine M. Millett, Ann M. Killenbeck*

Scholars often write and speak about the 1,820 or so four-year colleges and universities as if they are a single homogeneous class that shares equally the responsibility for the postsecondary instruction of the nation's students. Such is the case with Historically Black Colleges and Universities (HBCUs). The 105 four-year HBCUs (60 public and 45 private) are frequently written and spoken about as if they fit neatly into a single category. Yet there are both public and private HBCUs, and although most are small liberal arts undergraduate institutions, their physical plants and enrollments are large, medium, and small. Indeed, some have a broad range of degree programs at both the undergraduate and graduate levels.

The first public HBCU to be founded was Cheney College (1838), with Lincoln University (1854) the first private not far behind. These HBCUs represent only 2.5 percent of the four-year institutions of higher education in the country. They are all located in nineteen southern and southern border states. The private HBCUs are small (fewer than five thousand students) or midsized (five thousand to ten thousand students) higher education institutions. Only two private HBCUs have enrollments that exceed five thousand students, and fifteen more have enrollments greater than fifteen hundred students.

Throughout much of their history, HBCUs have had the primary responsibility for educating African Americans. These colleges and univer-

NEW DIRECTIONS FOR HIGHER EDUCATION, no. 108, Winter 1999 © Jossey-Bass Publishers

sities claim 3.3 percent (220,982) of the nation's 6.8 million undergraduates who enroll in four-year colleges and universities. Yet they account for 26.4 percent (191,158) of the 723,326 total African American undergraduate students enrolled in the nation's colleges and universities. Of the 191,158 African American undergraduates enrolled in HBCUs in 1996, 68.1 percent (130,177) attended public HBCUs and 30.8 percent (60,981) attended private HBCUs. African American students comprise 86.5 percent of the enrollment of the public HBCUs and 94.7 percent in the privates. HBCUs conferred approximately 2.5 percent (29,562) of the 1.17 million bachelor's degrees awarded in 1996. HBCUs awarded 28.3 percent (25,286) of the 89,412 bachelor's degrees awarded to African Americans in 1996. Of the 25,286 bachelor's degrees awarded to African Americans by HBCUs in 1996, 64.2 percent (16,236) were awarded by public HBCUs and 35.8 percent (9,050) by private HBCUs.

HBCUs once had the predominant role of providing the intellectual and social development for African Americans at the collegiate level. This role appears to be as important today as it has been throughout the past century and a half. Among all four-year colleges and universities, Howard University, Clark Atlanta University, Hampton University, and Spelman College are the four leading recipients of college admissions scores from African American examinees each year (College Board, 1998). Howard University, Spelman College, Xavier University, and Morehouse College are consistently among the top ten producers of African American medical school students and among the top twenty colleges and universities whose African American bachelor's degree recipients receive doctorates in the life, physical, computer, and engineering sciences.

Private HBCUs, like the vast share of other private colleges and universities that depend on tuition as the primary source of revenue, rely on student enrollment, retention, and progression as stable sources of revenue. Consequently, these are critical indicators of efficiency and effectiveness. In addition, enrollment, retention, and progression rates reveal the level of commitment and confidence that students have in colleges and universities, especially private institutions, where the price is typically relatively high. As one of the smallest sectors of American higher education, the forty-six private four-year HBCUs are heavily dependent on enrollment, retention, and progression as well as the most important by-products of institutional commitment: public confidence and alumni support. According to 1997 data, the private HBCUs have over ten thousand living alumni who contribute over $15 million each year (United Negro College Fund, 1998). This is an indication of the value and importance of ensuring that the students who enroll are retained and graduate.

Because private HBCUs have significantly lower endowments (average around $705,000) and tuition rates (average around $6,600) than predominantly white liberal arts colleges that are similar in size and mission, the institutional resources available to them are limited, demonstrating the somewhat difficult circumstances and environments in which they function and the challenges that they face. Despite their inability to compete in terms of resources with predominantly white liberal arts colleges, HBCUs continue to thrive and offer great value to some of the most disadvantaged African American students and families in the nation. Private HBCUs are the primary source of postsecondary education for economically disadvantaged African American students (those whose families have a total annual income of less than $25,000). Over 98 percent of the private HBCU students receive need-based federal financial aid. More than one-third of students enrolled in United Negro College Fund (UNCF) institutions, a national organization of thirty-nine private HBCUs, come from families with a total annual income of less than $25,000. In contrast, students from families with an income less than $25,000 comprise only 20 percent of those students attending all private nonsectarian colleges nationally.

Another challenge that HBCUs face is that their students generally receive less academic preparation prior to college than their counterparts throughout the rest of the nation's four-year colleges. The most frequent reminder is the comparison of average SAT scores for students entering HBCUs with those of students at other colleges and universities.

While much of the nation has only recently come to see retention as an important issue, private HBCUs have been working for decades to create cultures where retention is everyone's business: that of administrators, faculty, and individual students. For students entering college in 1989, a higher percentage of African Americans (43.2 percent) attending HBCUs persisted to the next academic level on time, compared with their African American counterparts attending majority institutions (33.7 percent) (Nettles and Perna, 1997). In addition, 45.1 percent of African Americans attending HBCUs (1989 cohort), compared with 43.5 percent of African Americans at majority institutions, attained bachelor's degrees within five years of initially enrolling (Nettles and Perna, 1997). Even at these rates, however, HBCUs recognize the need for higher retention and graduation rates. As higher education examines how it might improve student outcomes, it can benefit from the experiences of a few private HBCUs that, with the support of a philanthropic organization, brought their entire academic community together to tackle their challenges in student retention.

## The Pew Charitable Trusts Black Colleges Programs

The Pew Charitable Trusts have long supported the work of historically black colleges and universities. The Trusts' First Black Colleges Program began in 1982 with an award of $8.35 million in grants to fourteen private HBCUs and three support organizations. From 1987 to 1991, the Trusts' Second Black Colleges Program supported thirteen institutions in their efforts to improve science education and to construct and renovate buildings, for a total of $8.88 million.

In a 1992 meeting of private HBCU presidents hosted by the Trusts, the presidents identified student retention to graduation as being among the most important issues to address. In response, the Trusts committed a $4.4 million grant in 1993 to initiate the Third Black Colleges Program, a five-year program administered by the Southern Education Foundation (SEF) in Atlanta, Georgia.

Recognizing that no single solution will address student retention at all campuses, the Third Black Colleges Program was designed to allow participating colleges to plan and implement programs and strategies that would further their own efforts to increase student engagement and retention and to assist the participating colleges and universities to succeed in graduating a larger share of the students whom they admit as freshmen. The colleges were encouraged to introduce methods that each believed would be most beneficial to its unique circumstances and environment. Building on decades of effort by the colleges to foster a sense of community and responsibility, the Third Black Colleges Program asked each institution to design academic support services, professional development opportunities, or incentives programs. Each institution was asked to consider each of the following issues in their planning:

- Assess past and current practices, identifying what worked and what had not.
- Develop a strategic plan for systemic change that would become part of regular routines and behaviors.
- Engage in joint planning across academic departments.
- Examine the motivation behind student performance: why students achieve, why they persist, and why they drop out.
- Develop strategies, involving faculty, that focus on students' academic and social integration within the college.
- Assign both a project director and an evaluation coordinator who would take responsibility for creating a new institutional database or enhancing an existing one.
- Participate in two meetings of the Third Black Colleges Program participants each year to meet colleagues from other institutions, share with the other participating institutions their successful practices, and benefit from meeting with external experts on program implementation and evaluation. (The program also provided funds for project directors to visit each other's campuses.)

The proposals of ten of the fifteen institutions were accepted, and implementation grants ranging between $240,000 and $290,000 were awarded for the period July 1994 to June 1998. Following Vincent Tinto's (1987) theory of student retention, the ten institutions in the Third Black Colleges Program linked their programs to Tinto's premise that retention is closely tied to students' intellectual and social development and that involvement and commitment to the institution are key ingredients of student development. Satisfying and rewarding academic encounters in classrooms and with faculty mentors outside class lead to greater student integration and retention.

## Design of Individual Programs

The ten participating private HBCUs employed a variety of approaches in designing initiatives to increase their retention rates. Each effort, however, embodied one or more of three basic principles: building cooperative learning communities, encouraging faculty development as an impetus to student learning, and providing nonfinancial student incentives to stay in college. (The funds could not be used to provide student financial aid.)

**Dillard University.** Dillard University was founded in 1869 in New Orleans, Louisiana, and enrolls approximately 1,550 students. Dillard established four residential freshman learning communities of twenty-five students each. Two communities focus on developmental skills in reading, mathematics, English, and speech. The students selected were both economically disadvantaged and had college admissions test scores that suggested that they had a higher risk of dropping out before graduating than other entering students. The other two residential learning communities offer nondevelopmental courses in mathematics, English, world history, and natural sciences. Students who agree to join the learning communities attend Dillard's summer school prior to their regular freshman fall term. The students are given a stipend that makes forgoing summer employment feasible.

A group of faculty, who restructured their courses along common themes, serves each community. Weekly meetings focus on academic progress and problems that students are encountering, study skills, time organization, and test-taking skills development. This continuing contact over the freshman year allows students to discuss their problems openly as they are occurring and get assistance as the need arises.

**Fisk University.** Fisk University was founded in 1867 in Nashville, Tennessee, and enrolls approximately 765 students. Fisk reorganized its tutoring program to stress community building through cooperative learning. Upper-division students who have demonstrated academic achievement in the particular subject serve as student tutors. Substantial faculty involvement has expanded the number of students in the program, transforming it from a little-known service to a thriving enterprise.

Tutorial rooms are situated in the main classroom buildings, where student traffic makes it convenient for students to schedule appointments. An administrative assistant coordinates the program and organizes regular tutorial schedules.

**Hampton University.** Hampton University was founded in 1868 in Hampton, Virginia, and enrolls approximately 5,700 students. Hampton has placed special emphasis on student character and moral development, as exemplified in the Code of Conduct that each student and faculty member must agree to observe. Hampton established an extensive student counseling program for freshman and sophomores, although juniors and seniors can use its services too. The counseling programs were tailored to address problems that the younger students experience, such as separation from home and family, learning how to adopt to academic and social life, and issues of dating and sexuality.

For the Third Black Colleges Program, the university introduced the Faculty Development Advisor (FDA) Program as part of a larger culture that is supportive of student development. FDAs are trained in workshops on student concerns, academic program information and administrative regulations, and learning styles and time management. They meet monthly to discuss what works—and what does not.

In the fall semester, FDAs primarily assist with student advising and registration and serve as volunteer instructors in "University 101: The Individual and Life," a required, semester-long freshman orientation course. In the spring, each FDA advises five to fifteen first-year students on academic probation, organizes and monitors student study habits, leads small discussion groups, and joins students in informal social activities.

**Howard University.** Howard University was founded in 1867 in Washington, D.C., and enrolls approximately 10,450 students. Howard's Faculty Development Program works to create effective, efficient, and responsible instructors. At its inception, eleven experienced professors served as mentors to assistant professors and graduate teaching assistants, informally sharing their knowledge of teaching techniques, making efforts to improve syllabi, and sitting in to observe each other's courses.

Over seventy faculty members have joined workshops held during the summer, featuring guest speakers and covering such issues of importance to young faculty as the multiple roles that effective teachers must play, the need to pursue values and professionalism, and ways to address out-of-classroom obstacles to student learning. Each workshop is followed by a discussion session on professional roles and responsibilities.

**Johnson C. Smith University.** Johnson C. Smith University was founded in 1867 in Charlotte, North Carolina, and enrolls approximately 1,350 students. Most faculty members serve as mentors to students at Johnson Smith. Under a curriculum entitled "The Master Student" designed by the university's Center for Teaching and Learning, faculty mentors meet with freshmen weekly, as well as at intermittent academic skills workshops. The university distributes weekly newsletters to remind the mentors to assign a tutor to students who are on probation, attend the Founder's Day convocation with their students, and ensure that students complete community service requirements.

The mentors attend workshops to review advising methods, practice with role-playing techniques, and plan activities tailored to individual student needs. Some mentors invite students to accompany them to academic conferences; others take students to social events. Periodically the center plans campuswide presentations to share mentoring experiences. To date, faculty mentors have served over four hundred students. The weekly orientation sessions especially seem to contribute to students' sense of belonging to the university.

**Morehouse College.** Morehouse College, a male institution, was founded in 1867 in Atlanta, Georgia, and enrolls approximately 3,000 students. It sponsors a six-week, intensive summer program for seventy-five students with marginal academic preparation relative to students in U.S. four-year colleges and universities. The summer program is open to students, but is required of prospective students who are invited to participate and plan to matriculate at Morehouse in the fall. The summer program provides these students the chance to refine their skills in mathematics, English, and reading; increase their intellectual development; and build a sense of community. Although the college charges each student two thousand dollars to participate, need-based scholarships are available, and the vast majority of the students are eligible.

In addition to improving academic preparation, the program attempts to influence students to recognize the importance of academic success and a college education. Many of the students were raised in environments where their peers devalue academic achievement. To counter this problem, academically successful upperclassmen live in the dormitories with freshmen and serve as counselors and tutors. As positive role models, they are available on a one-to-four basis to provide the most convincing testimony that change is both possible and desirable.

**Rust College.** Rust College was founded in 1866 in Holly Springs, Mississippi, and enrolls approximately 875 students. During the first year, Rust provides tutoring, counseling, and remediation assistance for students.

All students are required to take internships related to their major field. This idea is that the internship permits students to apply classroom learning and provide students with an opportunity to see how earning a college degree will broaden their employment opportunities. The Career Development Center manages student internship placements, encouraging employers to become mentors—not just trainers—during the internship period. Placements of up to eight weeks earn students six hours of academic credit. Internships usually occur in the student's junior or senior year to ensure that they have the skills necessary to make a contribution to the chosen company and better appreciate how the experience will benefit their careers. Following the internship, the employer submits an evaluation of the student's mastery of specific skills and competencies. The student adds a self-appraisal, and then the academic advisers use both evaluations to decide on a grade for the student.

**Spelman College.** Spelman College was founded as a women's college in 1881 in Atlanta, Georgia, and enrolls approximately 1,950 students. Teaching and advising constitute central roles for Spelman faculty. By embracing this dual function, faculty members are able to identify students with academic problems at an early stage and intervene quickly.

The Learning Resources Center, established as the linchpin of the Spelman Third Black Colleges Program initiative, builds on this high degree of faculty involvement in all aspects of campus life. It offers academic advisement, tutoring, and instruction in study techniques.

Under its aegis, the Counseling Center helps reorient students who have lost sight of why they enrolled, the Writing Center works to assist students to develop their communications skills, and the Peer Tutoring Program recruits and trains qualified students to assist fellow students in a variety of academic disciplines. Faculty notify the academic dean when students are in trouble and need follow-up. This wide range of measures keeps students involved and on the road to retention.

**Tougaloo College.** Tougaloo College was founded in 1869 in Tougaloo, Mississippi, and enrolls approximately 900 students. Using a decentralized approach, Tougaloo has placed responsibility for retention on the individual academic departments. Over 80 percent of the college's faculty participate in department-based workshops designed to help improve their advising and teaching skills. The Committee on Faculty/Student Interaction notes that more faculty now make time to advise students and that they show a better understanding of what motivates undergraduates.

Tougaloo also sponsors faculty who participate in national advising and retention workshops. Once trained, they serve as a corps of trainers for their colleagues. During the summer, faculty can participate in a two-day training session on advising and attend periodic workshops conducted by the Center for Advising and Instruction.

**Xavier University of Louisiana.** Xavier University of Louisiana was founded in 1915 in New Orleans, Louisiana, and enrolls approximately 3,500 students. Xavier is the only African American Catholic college in the United States. Today fewer than 50 percent of the students are Catholic, and the overwhelming majority of the faculty are not members of a religious order, although the university still stresses spiritual and moral values such as honesty, integrity, discipline, and service.

Many Xavier students are the first in their family to attend college, and three-quarters of the student body is on financial aid. As a result of these societal factors, most students enter with poor academic preparation. But the seriousness with which Xavier takes teaching is seen by the fact that faculty promotion and tenure are based primarily on teaching ability.

The Mathematics Laboratory and the Academic Support Programs are cornerstones of the Xavier program developed with Trusts' funding. The Math Lab provides help from faculty members, peer tutors, and math software; the math faculty members volunteer one or two hours each week. During its first three years, students visited the lab almost seven thousand times, and the percentage of students passing the Collegiate Assessment of Academic Proficiency Test rose from 65 to 76.

The Academic Support Program involves roughly 10 percent of the student body as tutors, working with those who are on academic probation or shown to be at risk by midsemester. Students who received the program's tutoring showed a remarkable drop in the percentage on strict probation— from 74 percent in the fall of 1996 to 32 percent in the spring of 1997.

## Evaluation

Evaluation, both internal and external, was an integral part of the Third Black Colleges Program, with approximately 15 percent of the resources allocated for the overall project earmarked for evaluation. The external evaluation was designed with the dual purpose of monitoring the overall success of the projects and assisting the designated evaluator on each campus to plan and carry out internal institutional evaluations.

The consequence of this emphasis on evaluation is that each of the institutions developed evaluation plans, comprehensive databases for monitoring progress, instruments for assessing factors that contributed to progress, and periodic (annual) reports that presented their progress and outcomes. The periodic evaluation reports also provided the Trusts with the data and information needed to gauge the benefits from its investment in the Third Black Colleges Program.

## Database Development

Exhibit 4.1 presents the database design and elements that were recommended to the ten institutions. The data are predominantly student background characteristics, performance indicators, attitudes, and behaviors. Also shown are their retention and degree progress.

One of the purposes of the Trusts' initiative was to assist each college and university to create or improve its existing institutional database to enable it to track retention, progression, and graduation rates quickly and accurately and to evaluate academic success initiatives. When designed and well implemented, such databases can substantially strengthen an institution's capacity to intervene on behalf of its students.

Prior to the Trusts' initiative, most of the institutions described their databases as uncentralized, uncoordinated, and difficult to use. In addition, many were collecting a very limited range of data. For example, Johnson C. Smith University notes that its database did not contain variables to assess demographic data and prior educational histories on matriculates.

During the Third Black Colleges Program, each college or university established a team of key campus staff to review and suggest modifications to the database.

The HBCUs reported lessons about database development that may be useful to other colleges and universities. Howard University suggested that changes in the database must be institutionalized. Officials observed that database users must appreciate the importance of timely and accurate data and routinely adjust their approach to enhance the long-range usefulness

## Exhibit 4.1. Retention and Progression Database Design for Third Black Colleges Program

1. Demographics of entering freshman class
   - Age
   - Sex
   - Race
   - Socio-economic status
   - Parents' education
   - Sibling's education

2. Academic background characteristics
   - High school grade point average
   - High school courses taken
   - Entering SAT or ACT scores
   - Academic awards received

3. Financial characteristics
   - Parents' income
   - Amount of financial aid received
   - Scholarships
   - Federal grants
   - State grants
   - Federal loans
   - Institutional loans
   - Other

4. Student attitudes, behaviors, motivation, and opinions
   - Student satisfaction with the following:
     - Financial assistance
     - Admissions process
     - Courses
     - Registration process
     - Faculty
   - Academic advising about courses to choose

5. College student retention
   - The percent of students in each class who returned to the institution in each term after initial enrollment
   - A comparison of the characteristics and academic performance of students who are retained compared to those students who drop-out

6. Progression rate
   - Number of 1993 full-time freshmen who return as sophomores in 1994 (this would be repeated for each cohort in every year)
   - Number of credit hours each student accumulated per term of enrollment from that point of entering through present

7. Student performance in college
   - Student cumulative grade point average
   - Student grade point average by major field
   - 1994 freshman student performance on the examinations in their major field

of the data to the university. Rust College recommended that database development include annual or semiannual checklists that can be sent to individual offices, departments, and areas of the campus to solicit new information to include in the database.

Of the nine participating institutions that refined or upgraded their database system through the Trusts' initiative (Xavier University's system was already fully functioning), all agreed or strongly agreed that these efforts enabled them to track student retention, progression, and graduation rates accurately. All nine institutions also agreed that the time and resources they devoted to the development or refinement of their institutional database were worth it.

As part of the project, the ten colleges agreed on an annual evaluation plan and some common definitions for key concepts that were the focus of the initiative, by which they would periodically measure and report their progress:

Retention: Students who remain in school and do not drop out or transfer. An institution's retention rate is the percentage of an entering class that remains in school.
Progression: Students who progress from one academic level to the next. An institution's progression rate is the percentage of an entering class that moves from freshman to sophomore status, from sophomore to junior status, and so forth, in consecutive academic years.
Graduation: Students who graduate from the college. An institution's graduation rate is the percentage of an entering class that graduates. (Only four-year graduation rates are available to date for the Third Black Colleges Program institutions. On a national basis, many students take five to six years to graduate from college.)

## Improvement in Performance Indicators

After five years of effort, the freshman retention rates increased for nine of the ten HBCUs participating in the initiative (Figure 4.1). The rates are the percentage of first-time, full-time freshmen who return after their freshman year. (The largest dropout usually occurs from freshman to sophomore year.) This, and second-year rates, are widely believed to be the most critical periods for long-term retention and graduation. Fisk University experienced the largest increase; its freshman retention rate rose from 83 percent for the 1994 freshman cohort to 94 percent for the 1997 freshman cohort.

The data on student progression from freshman to sophomore status show slightly less dramatic gains (Figure 4.2). The progression rate at six of the HBCUs increased, while one progression rate remained stable. Again Fisk University experienced the largest increase; its freshman-to-sophomore progression rate rose from 64 percent for the 1994 cohort to 72 percent for the 1997 cohort. Spelman College, the institution with the highest

**Figure 4.1. Freshman-to-Sophomore Retention Rates for Students Entering in 1994 and 1997**

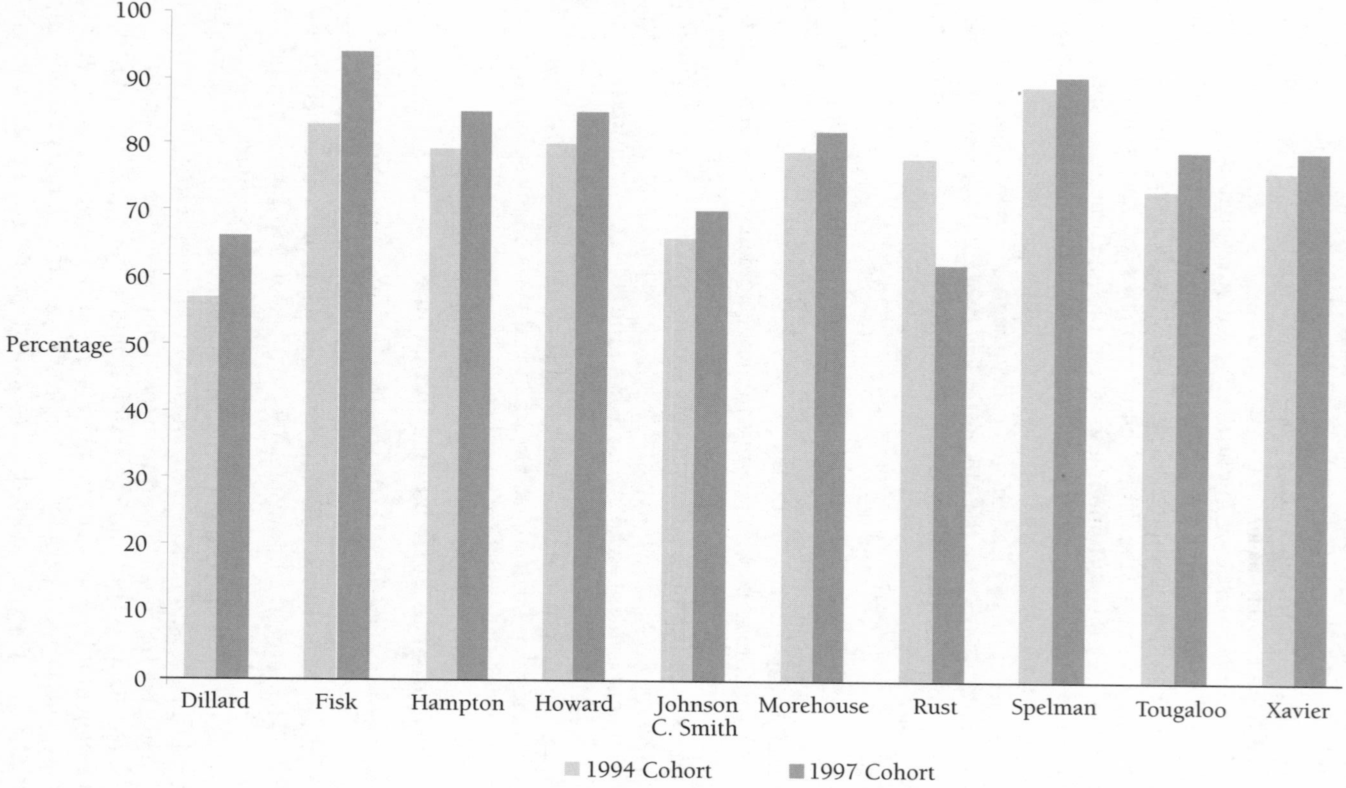

■ 1994 Cohort  ■ 1997 Cohort

**Figure 4.2. Freshman-to-Sophomore Progression Rates for Students Entering in 1994 and 1997**

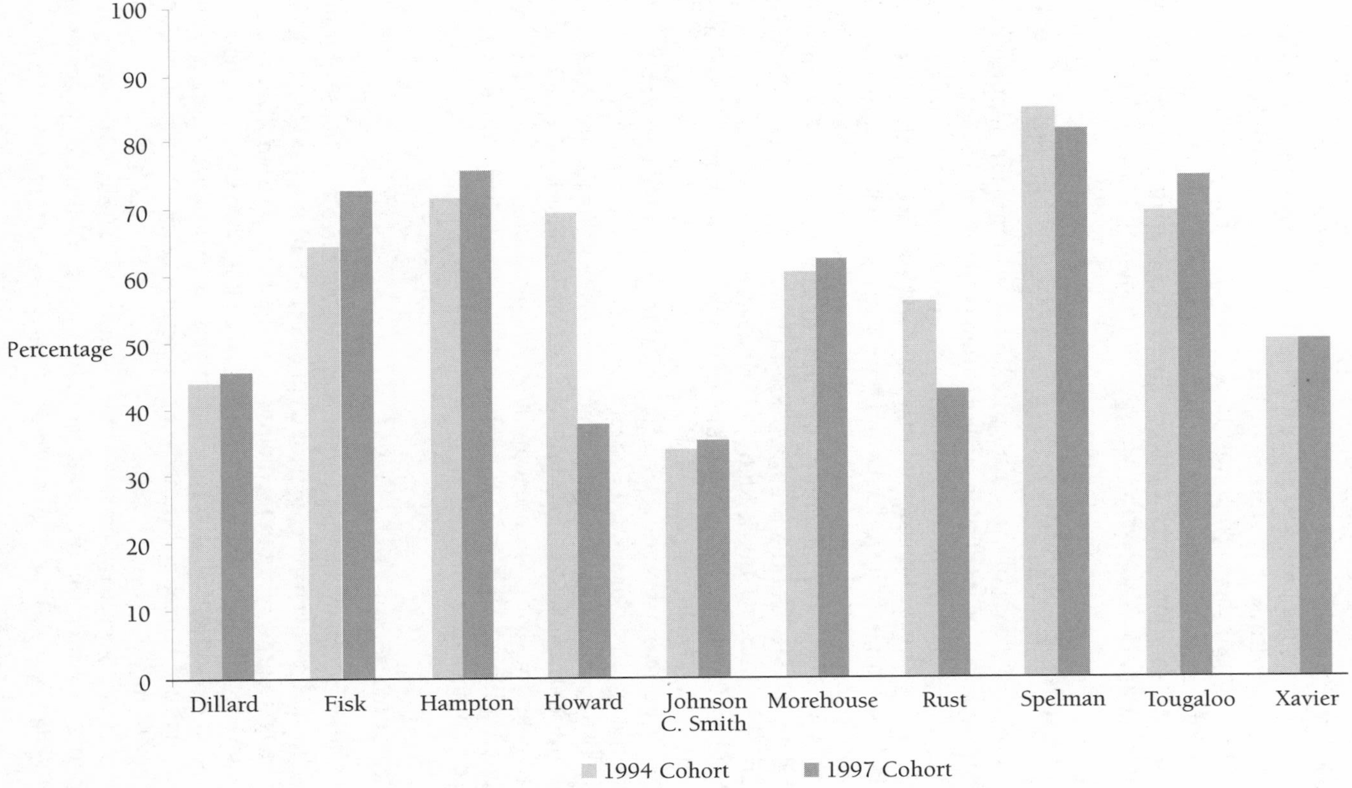

long-term retention and graduation rates, has a 90 percent freshman retention rate and above 80 percent freshman progression rate.

Finally, the four-year graduation rate increased for seven of the participating institutions (Figure 4.3). The largest gains occurred at Fisk—from 30 percent of the 1989 cohort to 36 percent of the 1994 cohort—and at Spelman—from 60 percent of the 1989 cohort to 66 percent of the 1994 cohort. The Third Black Colleges Program anticipates further gains in the graduation rates after a five-year period (ending in May 1999).

## Enhanced Collegiality

Another purpose of the Trusts' initiative was to provide opportunities for the participating institutions to learn from both experts in the field and their colleagues through national workshops and site visits to other campuses.

These institutions agreed that the workshops were particularly helpful in broadening their understanding of national retention and achievement initiatives. Workshop topics over the years covered such issues as "What We Know from the Literature—Implications for Action," "Academic Counseling: The Role of the Faculty," "Freshman Year Initiatives," "Recruitment and Retention of Black Males," "Bridge Programs," "Financial Aid and Career Counseling," and "Building Learning Communities: What the Institution Can Do."

The Trusts' initiative was successful in generating collaborative activity. Each college or university made between ten and twenty-five telephone calls to peer institutions, and many made site visits to other campuses to learn firsthand about their progress. A few universities created their own vehicles for sharing information; for example, Hampton University hosted an Enrollment Management Institute that was widely attended by key staff from other HBCUs.

## Useful Lessons

Because so many factors combine to determine an individual student's achievement over the course of a college curriculum, gauging the success of any program takes time. Judging whether the effects are confined to one class of students or are systemic takes even longer to observe. Higher education institutions should therefore undertake a sustained effort and remain committed to retention initiatives over several years in order to realize positive results.

It is difficult to assess the long-range effects of the program at this point. However, the implementation of the Third Black Colleges Program and its early successes have already provided several useful lessons:

Student retention interventions work best when they are integral to the entire college community, which views them as being part of the institution's mission and vitality.

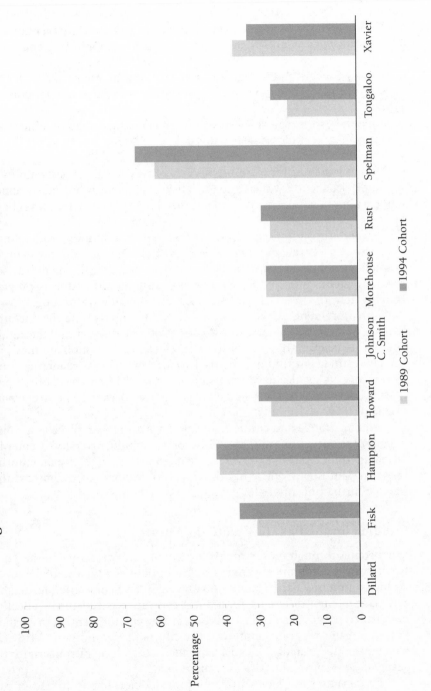

**Figure 4.3. Four-Year Graduation Rates, 1989 and 1994 Cohorts**

Faculty development with a focus on student learning is essential.

Early identification of at-risk students is key for effective intervention.

Database development is a prerequisite to effective monitoring and evaluation.

Individual colleges and universities can benefit from interaction with similar institutions during the process of implementing student retention programs.

Retention efforts are most successful when everyone—faculty, administrators, staff, and students—is involved.

A fundamental measure of success for any program is its ability to become permanently woven into the fabric of an institution and sustained. Some of the most innovative models developed by participating schools have passed this test.

Several institutions were able to secure external funding from foundations and the federal government. Support from the Lilly Endowment, for example, has enabled Hampton University's Faculty Development Advisors program to continue, and Fisk University's campuswide tutoring program benefits from the U.S. Department of Education's Title III funding.

Other programs are being sustained through funds from the operating budgets of their own institutions. At Tougaloo, the director and the administrative assistant of the Center for Advising and Instruction are now paid from unrestricted institutional funds. Howard University uses internal funds to continue its faculty development workshops. Morehouse College pays outside consultants to train the staff of student services to be more customer oriented.

Administrative and cultural changes have also taken place as a consequence of the retention initiative. Johnson C. Smith University's Center for Teaching and Learning is now responsible for the university's mentoring program, and Rust College has developed two sophomore seminars that provide further incentives for students to remain in school.

## Building on the Past to Create the Future

What comes through most strongly in virtually every instance in the Third Black Colleges Program experience is that initiatives with a combination of strong community focus, faculty involvement, and committed leadership can make a major difference for academically at-risk students by affecting not just retention rates but their entire learning environment. Perhaps most important, the program reinforced the efforts of the individual HBCUs, which have traditionally shown a particularly high level of concern for the academic and spiritual health of their students.

Furthermore, the Trusts' initiative provided new opportunities for participating institutions to learn from their colleagues and from experts in the field through national workshops and site visits to other campuses. Institutional leaders and program coordinators polled at all participating schools agreed or strongly agreed that the national workshops broadened their understanding of both retention and achievement.

## References

College Board. Unpublished tabulations. New York, 1998.

Nettles, M. T., and Perna, L. W. *The African American Education Data Book: Volume 1: Higher and Adult Education.* Fairfax, Va.: Frederick D. Patterson Research Institute of the College Fund/UNCF, 1997.

Pew Charitable Trusts. *Historically Black Colleges and Universities Take a Closer Look at Student Retention.* N.p.: Pew Charitable Trusts, 1999. Report, available online at http://www.pewtrusts.com.

Tinto, V. *Leaving College: Rethinking the Causes and Cures of Student Attrition.* Chicago: University of Chicago Press, 1987.

United Negro College Fund. *The 1997 United Negro College Fund Statistical Report.* Fairfax, Va: United Negro College Fund, 1998.

Wagener, U., and Nettles, M. "It Takes a Community to Educate Students: How Three HBCU's Succeed at Retention." *Change,* 1998, *30* (2), 18–25.

MICHAEL T. NETTLES *is professor of education at the University of Michigan, Ann Arbor.*

URSULA WAGENER *is adjunct associate professor of higher education at the University of Pennsylvania.*

CATHERINE M. MILLETT *is assistant research scientist at the University of Michigan, Ann Arbor.*

ANN M. KILLENBECK *is a doctoral candidate at the University of Michigan, Ann Arbor.*

5

*Two methods for calculating expected retention and graduation rates for multicampus university systems are presented. One requires the decomposition of the student population into mutually exclusive subgroups based on relevant student characteristics. The other uses logistic regression to calculate the probabilities of student success; this approach is shown to be superior, particularly if there are more than two or three student variables to be included in the analysis.*

# Modeled Retention and Graduation Rates: Calculating Expected Retention and Graduation Rates for Multicampus University Systems

*Gary Blose*

Increasingly colleges and universities are being asked to demonstrate performance and show the degree to which they achieve selected elements of their institutional mission. At the federal level, the recent student-right-to-know legislation is probably one of the more obvious examples, but in many states the greatest impact in the public sector has come from state governments that are mandating performance indicator programs to justify their significant investment in higher education. Often these assessment initiatives have resulted in a direct linkage between performance and funding. The notion of performance-based funding is gaining widespread support and has become increasingly popular with legislators and governors as a means of rewarding good practice and punishing inefficiencies and waste. The theory is fine, but in practice the problems derive from our inability to assess accurately many of the most important aspects of the educational process and the institutional mission. Most people recognize a legitimate need for accountability and realize that the fiscal and societal pressures to improve educational performance are likely to increase, at least in the foreseeable future. Accepting this, those engaged in institutional research must begin to devise better measures of institutional accomplishment, particularly in those performance areas that are especially important and where current practice is inadequate.

Certain elements of the educational process seem to lend themselves to easy quantification, and as a result, these are among the first things requested

New Directions for Higher Education, no. 108, Winter 1999  © Jossey-Bass Publishers

when evaluating institutional performance. One of the more common variables that fall into this category is graduation rates. Comparing graduation rates among colleges might seem easy to do: define a common entering cohort, give the students sufficient time to complete the academic requirements of their degree program, and calculate the percentage that received their degree. Although it would seem relatively straightforward, any comparison must be predicated on the assumption that the institutions should have the same or similar graduation rates. If it turns out that the rates are not the same, the institution with the higher percentage will generally be presumed to be doing the better job. This conclusion may be faulty, however, and recognizing this and dealing with its ramifications is the subject examined in this chapter.

A whole host of factors will determine whether a particular student will graduate. Some of these conditions are directly attributable to the institution or college, but most are associated more with the individual student. If student-related factors were uniformly distributed across all campuses, it would then be much more reasonable to expect all colleges to have the same or at least similar graduation results. This is a fallacious assumption, however, because of the extraordinary amount of variability among institutions in virtually every aspect of their students' characteristics. Therefore, when the typical student enrolled at two institutions differs significantly with respect to the traits that are known to be associated with graduation, the more selective institution would be expected to have the better graduation rate. Simply stated, the institution with the "better" students should have the higher graduation rate. Consequently, if comparison is to be equitable, there must be an adjustment for what might be designated "student academic potential." The problem of comparing graduation rates therefore becomes one of determining and then comparing only those colleges that are equally selective or devising a way of equating institutions regardless of the actual characteristics of the students enrolled.

Comparing only similarly selective institutions is an option, but it severely restricts the number of comparisons that can be made, and it is not nearly as intriguing as the alternative: adjusting the graduation rates for student characteristics. Ideally it would be best if there were some mechanism or formula that would allow a comparison of virtually any institution with any other and do it in such a way that there is a truly meaningful basis for the comparison. In effect, we would want to create an equating system that rescales graduation results, so relating one to another without massive qualification is possible.

What I propose here is not a way of equating colleges but a way of developing a reasonable set of performance expectations, given the academic and demographic characteristics of the students enrolled. To produce this, the initial requirement is to determine a set of variables that are significantly associated or correlated with college graduation. Not only should these variables be associated with graduation, but they should also be determined solely by the individual student's background and not be a characteristic of the institution at which he or she is enrolled. Further, it would be preferable if the variables represented things that are readily available at an institution as part of the routine student application or registration process.

Once discovered, the relationship between these variables and graduation could be used to establish a predictive model that is largely independent of the specific institution that the student attends. Whenever possible, any effects due to the institution (as opposed to the individual) are to be removed. Institutional effects can never be totally eliminated, because the output measure being used (the granting of a college degree) is intrinsically tied to the institutions used in the analysis. This institution-specific effect, however, will be inversely related to the number of institutions used in the analysis. The relationship between the predictors and college graduation needs to be established across as many institutions as possible, so that the influence of the factors that are directly attributable to the institution, rather than the student as an individual, is kept to a minimum. Consequently, the more broadly based the data are, in terms of both the institutions and the students, the more generalizable will be the results.

## Estimation of Expected Values

If a probability of graduation could be assigned to each student at the time of initial enrollment, it would then become a simple arithmetic exercise to calculate the expected number of students who should graduate within a specified period of time. For example, if an institution had an entering freshman class of ten students and knew that the probability of graduating within four years was 0.7 for three of them, and five had a probability of 0.6, and the last two had a probability of 0.5, and it wanted to predict the number of students who would actually graduate four years hence, the best prediction would be the sum of the individual probabilities:

Expected graduation = $(3 \times 0.7) + (5 \times 0.6) + (2 \times 0.5) = 6.1$.

Thus, about six students in the entering cohort should finish within four years. If the probabilities are at all realistic, then this calculation would give a reasonable projection. To extend the example, let us assume that there are only these three types of students (Types A, B, and C) and that the calculated probabilities are real and represent the average probability of graduating within four years, based on the performance of all baccalaureate institutions in the United States. If an institution knew the number of each student type enrolled, its expected graduation rate for each year over the past few years could be calculated and compared to the number of students actually graduated. If it turned out that students consistently outperformed the model, then this should be taken as a positive indicator that the institution is exceeding the national average and is ostensibly doing something right. On the other hand, if fewer of the students graduate than expected, this indicates the possibility of some institutional impediments to graduation. In either case, this exercise would allow a comparison against a standard that is not absolute but is tailored to the particular characteristics of the institution in question.

To illustrate, assume Type A students have an expected graduation rate of 0.7 irrespective of institution, and Type B students have a 0.6 rate, with Type C students graduating at 0.5. Institution XYZ admits only Type A's and graduates 65 percent of its students. Institution ABC enrolls only Type C's but graduates 60 percent of them. In a comparison only on the raw graduation rates, Institution XYZ prevails, because it graduated a greater proportion of students. If, however, the calculation factors in the type of students enrolled and how they fare after they enroll, Institution ABC would seem to be doing a much better job. Institution XYZ could contend that this was a function of a much more difficult curriculum—and it may even be correct. In any case if Institutions XYZ and ABC are going to be compared, it would be better to do so using a modeled expectation rather than the simple raw rates.

## The Variables and the Formula

Numerous studies have found that basic student characteristics such as gender, race, age, and family income are significantly correlated with both college graduation in general and length of time to degree (Pascarella and Terenzini, 1991). Combining these variables along with standard academic performance measures, such as the student's high school average, rank in high school, and standardized test scores (SAT/ACT), yields an excellent set of indicators that can be used to predict with a high degree of precision the likelihood of college graduation for students with known characteristics.

Following the rationale already established, there are a couple of statistical techniques available for estimating the probability of graduation based on gender, race, age, family income, SAT scores, high school rank, and high school average for some specified set of students. The easier of these to understand is to take each intersection of values for all variables included in the analysis (collapsing across institution) and then calculate the percentage graduating for each group. Then determine the number of each type of student enrolled at each institution, multiply this value by the percentage graduating, sum across groups, and arrive at an expected graduation figure. The grand total will always equal the sum of the corresponding actual values when the expected values are calculated using either of the methods suggested in this chapter. This fact will become useful later when indexes are developed to evaluate institutional performance.

To illustrate, assume that we have data on an initial cohort of full-time, first-time freshmen at three institutions and these students have had at least four years in which to graduate. To keep the example reasonably simple, only gender and high school average will be used. Table 5.1 provides the distribution of students by institution and trait. Table 5.2 recasts the data from Table 5.1 and shows the actual graduation rates, the expected graduation rates, and the difference for each cell at each college.

The following notation will be used to demonstrate the calculation algorithms:

$C_{ijk}$ = initial number of freshmen at institution $i$, gender $j$, and high school average $k$

$G_{ijk}$ = graduates from cohort at institution $i$, gender $j$, and high school average $k$

$E_{ijk}$ = expected number of graduates for institution $i$, gender $j$, and high school average $k$

$E_{ijk} = p_{ijk}C_{ijk}$

$p.jk = \sum_{1}^{i}G_{ijk} / \sum_{1}^{i}C_{ijk}$ = percentage of graduates

for gender $j$, high school average $k$

From this, the total number of expected graduates can be calculated for each institution using:

$$E_{i..} = \sum_{1}^{j}\sum_{1}^{k}E_{.jk}$$

From Table 5.1, the expected number of graduates at Institutions A, B, and C, respectively, would be:

$E_A$ = (.6327 × 33) + (.4504 × 185) + . . . 
        + (.5000 × 30) + . . . + (.0282 × 0) = 551.59

$E_B$ = (.6327 × 10) + (.4504 × 47) + . . . 
        + (.5000 × 4) + . . . + (.0282 × 0) = 280.86

$E_C$ = (.6327 × 6) + (.4504 × 30) + . . . 
        + (.5000 × 4) + . . . + (.0282 × 71) = 271.55

Comparing expected graduation with what actually happened:

|  | Actual | Expected | Ratio |
|---|---|---|---|
| Institution A | 508 | 552 | .92 |
| Institution B | 280 | 281 | .99 |
| Institution C | 316 | 271 | 1.16 |
| TOTAL | 1,104 | 1,104 | 1.00 |

## Table 5.1. Four-Year Graduation Rates for Full-Time, First-Time Students Enrolling in a Baccalaureate Degree Program, by Gender and High School Averages

| Gender and College | Entering Cohort and Number Graduating | High School Average | | | | | | All Students |
|---|---|---|---|---|---|---|---|---|
| | | Over 95 | 90–94 | 85–89 | 80–84 | 75–79 | Below 75 | |
| **Women** | | | | | | | | |
| College A | Cohort | 33 | 185 | 319 | 201 | 7 | 0 | 745 |
| | Graduates | 19 | 79 | 112 | 59 | 2 | 0 | 271 |
| | Percentage Graduates | 57.58 | 42.70 | 35.11 | 29.35 | 28.57 | 0.00 | 56.38 |
| College B | Cohort | 10 | 47 | 128 | 178 | 57 | 0 | 420 |
| | Graduates | 8 | 23 | 55 | 44 | 19 | 0 | 149 |
| | Percentage Graduates | 80.00 | 48.94 | 42.97 | 24.72 | 33.33 | 0.00 | 35.48 |
| College C | Cohort | 6 | 30 | 123 | 182 | 90 | 59 | 490 |
| | Graduates | 4 | 16 | 54 | 81 | 21 | 2 | 178 |
| | Percentage Graduates | 66.67 | 53.33 | 43.90 | 44.51 | 23.33 | 3.39 | 36.33 |
| All women | Cohort | 49 | 262 | 570 | 561 | 154 | 59 | 1,655 |
| | Graduates | 31 | 118 | 221 | 184 | 42 | 2 | 598 |
| | Percentage Graduates | 63.27 | 45.04 | 38.77 | 32.80 | 27.27 | 3.39 | 36.13 |
| **Men** | | | | | | | | |
| College A | Cohort | 30 | 179 | 304 | 127 | 10 | 0 | 650 |
| | Graduates | 15 | 66 | 101 | 54 | 1 | 0 | 237 |
| | Percentage Graduates | 50.00 | 36.87 | 33.22 | 42.52 | 10.00 | 0.00 | 36.46 |
| College B | Cohort | 4 | 48 | 112 | 127 | 55 | 0 | 346 |
| | Graduates | 3 | 22 | 49 | 40 | 17 | 0 | 131 |
| | Percentage Graduates | 75.00 | 45.83 | 43.75 | 31.50 | 30.91 | 0.00 | 37.86 |
| College C | Cohort | 4 | 32 | 99 | 105 | 91 | 71 | 402 |
| | Graduates | 1 | 17 | 41 | 56 | 21 | 2 | 138 |
| | Percentage Graduates | 25.00 | 53.13 | 41.41 | 53.33 | 23.08 | 2.82 | 34.33 |
| All men | Cohort | 38 | 259 | 515 | 359 | 156 | 71 | 1,398 |
| | Graduates | 19 | 105 | 191 | 150 | 39 | 2 | 506 |
| | Percentage Graduates | 50.00 | 40.54 | 37.09 | 41.78 | 25.00 | 2.82 | 36.19 |
| **Total** | | | | | | | | |
| College A | Cohort | 63 | 364 | 623 | 328 | 17 | 0 | 1,395 |
| | Graduates | 34 | 145 | 213 | 113 | 3 | 0 | 508 |
| | Percentage Graduates | 53.97 | 39.84 | 34.19 | 34.45 | 17.65 | 0.00 | 36.42 |
| College B | Cohort | 14 | 95 | 240 | 305 | 112 | 0 | 766 |
| | Graduates | 11 | 45 | 104 | 84 | 36 | 0 | 280 |
| | Percentage Graduates | 78.57 | 47.37 | 43.33 | 27.54 | 32.14 | 0.00 | 36.55 |
| College C | Cohort | 10 | 62 | 222 | 287 | 181 | 130 | 892 |
| | Graduates | 5 | 33 | 95 | 137 | 42 | 4 | 316 |
| | Percentage Graduates | 50.00 | 53.23 | 42.79 | 47.74 | 23.20 | 3.08 | 35.43 |
| Total | Cohort | 87 | 521 | 1,085 | 920 | 310 | 130 | 3,053 |
| | Graduates | 50 | 223 | 412 | 334 | 81 | 4 | 1,104 |
| | Percentage Graduates | 57.47 | 42.80 | 37.97 | 36.30 | 26.13 | 3.08 | 36.16 |

**Table 5.2. Actual and Expected Graduates with Difference
by College, Gender, and High School Average**

| Gender and College | Cohort and Actual Expected Graduates | High School Average | | | | | | All Students |
|---|---|---|---|---|---|---|---|---|
| | | Over 95 | 90–94 | 85–89 | 80–84 | 75–79 | Below 75 | |
| **Women** | | | | | | | | |
| College A | Cohort | 33 | 185 | 319 | 201 | 7 | 0 | 745 |
| | Actual Graduates | 19 | 79 | 112 | 59 | 2 | 0 | 271 |
| | Expected Graduates | 20.88 | 83.32 | 123.68 | 65.93 | 1.91 | 0.00 | 296 |
| | Difference (Actual − Expected) | −1.88 | −4.32 | −11.68 | -6.93 | 0.09 | 0.00 | −24.72 |
| College B | Cohort | 10 | 47 | 128 | 178 | 57 | 0 | 420 |
| | Actual Graduates | 8 | 23 | 55 | 44 | 19 | 0 | 149 |
| | Expected Graduates | 6.33 | 21.17 | 49.63 | 58.38 | 15.55 | 0.00 | 151 |
| | Difference (Actual − Expected) | 1.67 | 1.83 | 5.37 | -14.38 | 3.45 | 0.00 | −2.06 |
| College C | Cohort | 6 | 30 | 123 | 182 | 90 | 59 | 490 |
| | Actual Graduates | 4 | 16 | 54 | 81 | 21 | 2 | 178 |
| | Expected Graduates | 3.80 | 13.51 | 47.69 | 59.69 | 24.55 | 2.00 | 151 |
| | Difference (Actual − Expected) | 0.20 | 2.49 | 6.31 | 21.31 | −3.55 | 0.00 | 26.76 |
| All women | Cohort | 49 | 262 | 570 | 561 | 154 | 59 | 1,655 |
| | Actual Graduates | 31 | 118 | 221 | 184 | 42 | 2 | 598 |
| | Expected Graduates | 31.00 | 118.00 | 221.00 | 184.00 | 42.00 | 2.00 | 598 |
| Percentages (women) | | 63.27 | 45.04 | 38.77 | 32.80 | 27.27 | 3.39 | 36.13 |
| **Men** | | | | | | | | |
| College A | Cohort | 30 | 179 | 304 | 127 | 10 | 0 | 650 |
| | Actual Graduates | 15 | 66 | 101 | 54 | 1 | 0 | 237 |
| | Expected Graduates | 15.00 | 72.57 | 112.75 | 53.06 | 2.50 | 0.00 | 256 |
| | Difference (Actual − Expected) | 0.00 | −6.57 | −11.75 | 0.94 | -1.50 | 0.00 | −18.88 |
| College B | Cohort | 4 | 48 | 112 | 127 | 55 | 0 | 346 |
| | Actual Graduates | 3 | 22 | 49 | 40 | 17 | 0 | 131 |
| | Expected Graduates | 2.00 | 19.46 | 41.54 | 53.06 | 13.75 | 0.00 | 130 |
| | Difference (Actual − Expected) | 1.00 | 2.54 | 7.46 | -13.06 | 3.25 | 0.00 | 1.19 |
| College C | Cohort | 4 | 32 | 99 | 105 | 91 | 71 | 402 |
| | Actual Graduates | 1 | 17 | 41 | 56 | 21 | 2 | 138 |
| | Expected Graduates | 2.00 | 12.97 | 36.72 | 43.87 | 22.75 | 2.00 | 120 |
| | Difference (Actual − Expected) | −1.00 | 4.03 | 4.28 | 12.13 | −1.75 | 0.00 | 17.69 |
| All men | Cohort | 38 | 259 | 515 | 359 | 156 | 71 | 1,398 |
| | Actual Graduates | 19 | 105 | 191 | 150 | 39 | 2 | 506 |
| | Expected Graduates | 19.00 | 105.00 | 191.00 | 150.00 | 39.00 | 2.00 | 506 |
| Percentages (men) | | 50.00 | 40.54 | 37.09 | 41.78 | 25.00 | 2.82 | 36.19 |
| **Total** | | | | | | | | |
| College A | Cohort | 63 | 364 | 623 | 328 | 17 | 0 | 1,395 |
| | Actual Graduates | 34 | 145 | 213 | 113 | 3 | 0 | 508 |
| | Expected Graduates | 35.88 | 155.89 | 236.43 | 118.99 | 4.41 | 0 | 552 |
| | Difference (Actual − Expected) | −1.88 | −10.89 | −23.43 | −5.99 | −1.41 | 0.00 | −43.60 |
| College B | Cohort | 14 | 95 | 240 | 305 | 112 | 0 | 766 |
| | Actual Graduates | 11 | 45 | 104 | 84 | 36 | 0 | 280 |
| | Expected Graduates | 8.33 | 40.63 | 91.17 | 111.44 | 29.3 | 0 | 281 |
| | Difference (Actual − Expected) | 2.67 | 4.37 | 12.83 | −27.44 | 6.70 | 0.00 | −0.87 |
| College C | Cohort | 10 | 62 | 222 | 287 | 181 | 130 | 892 |
| | Actual Graduates | 5 | 33 | 95 | 137 | 42 | 4 | 316 |
| | Expected Graduates | 5.8 | 26.48 | 84.41 | 103.56 | 47.3 | 4 | 272 |
| | Difference (Actual − Expected) | −0.80 | 6.52 | 10.59 | 33.44 | −5.30 | 0.00 | 44.45 |
| Total | Cohort | 87 | 521 | 1,085 | 920 | 310 | 130 | 3,053 |
| | Actual Graduates | 50 | 223 | 412 | 334 | 81 | 4 | 1,104 |
| | Expected Graduates | 50.00 | 223.00 | 412.00 | 334.00 | 81.00 | 4.00 | 1,104 |
| Percentages (total) | | 57.47 | 42.80 | 37.97 | 36.30 | 26.13 | 3.08 | 36.16 |

Along with this, actual and expected graduation rates can be calculated:

|  | Actual Percentage | Expected Percentage |
|---|---|---|
| Institution A | 36.42 | 39.57 |
| Institution B | 36.55 | 36.68 |
| Institution C | 35.43 | 30.38 |

The three institutions have very similar actual graduation rates: 36.4 percent at Institution A, 36.6 percent at Institution B, and 35.4 percent at Institution C. Looking no further, it might be assumed that they are doing equally well at graduating students within four years—but they are not. Looking solely at actual rates, the institutions are within a percentage point, but after equating on gender and high school average, the spread increases dramatically to a little over 9 percent.

Consider first the distribution of students by high school average. Institution A is much more selective than the other two institutions, with Institution B being more selective than Institution C. While Institution A had the "best" students, Table 5.2 indicates that in virtually every cell, it failed to graduate the "expected" number of students. Institution C, on the other hand, began with students who had less academic potential but exceeded expectation in all but a few cells. Even when Institution C fell below expected rates in a particular cell, the difference from the actual was very small. Given the way students at these three institutions perform, the analysis indicates that Institution A would have had to graduate 39.6 percent of its students to be at the group average; this did not happen.

The expectation for Institutions B and C would be lower because the analysis indicates that institutions with their student profile should graduate fewer students in general than those at Institution A. In effect, norms are being developed and are based on the collective behavior of each group (irrespective of institution). These norms do not require any a priori assumptions about the institutions or the distribution of students by trait. All of the institutions included in the analysis contribute the performance of their students to the establishment of the norms. The only underlying assumption is that the behavior of the students included in the study reflects a reasonable standard of performance. This will generally be true if there are enough students and enough institutions to portray the general graduation patterns accurately. Are three institutions enough to produce valid results limited to a couple of explanatory variables (gender and high school average in our example)? As the number of variables increases, so must the number of students.

This is one of the problems with this approach. To get reasonable and stable estimates of the probabilities, there need to be a certain number of observations at each combination of traits. Obviously, the more variables placed in combination, the more difficult it will be to achieve the needed mass. For example, if Gender (two levels), High School Average (say six levels), High School Rank (five categories), Race (six categories), Age (three categories), and Family Income (five levels) at twenty colleges were used, we would have $2 \times 6 \times 5 \times 6 \times 3 \times 5 \times 20 = 108,000$ cells. Obviously, things get out of hand very quickly as the number of variables escalates. Some variables could be eliminated from the analysis; Age and High School Rank might be good candidates. Others could be consolidated: Race, for example, could become Underrepresented Minority and Other, or Family Income could be grouped Low Income and Other. But even after such consolidations, a tremendous number of students would be needed to make it work. Actually, using anything more than two or three variables becomes unwieldy and probably requires another model. Fortunately one exists, as we will see below, but this should not be taken as a dismissal of the methodology just discussed. The presented approach works quite well if the only goal is to adjust for a few variables. Even if including more variables is desired, understanding the basic concepts shown here will lay the groundwork for the approach that is about to be developed.

In every preceding hypothetical example presented, the more selective institution endured the worst of the comparisons. In actual practice, this would not happen and is simply a contrivance to show that high raw rates do not necessarily translate into the best modeled rates. Experience in applying this and similar methodologies to institutions in the State University of New York (SUNY) system has not shown this pattern. In fact, any bias would probably go in the other direction. Generally institutions that attract the better academically prepared students must be providing an environment that is attractive to students who have the most enrollment options when selecting a college. The quality of this environment, along with a high level of academic expectation imposed on every student, even those who might fall below the local norm, actually serves to raise the performance of the most highly selective institutions. In effect, if students are operating in an environment that expects them to do well and fosters the notion that they should graduate, they are much more likely to comply, regardless of their prior academic history. In short, students tend to respond to the expectations of the environment.

## Logistic Regression

Institutional graduation is associated with certain demographic patterns, and it is useful to capitalize on known relationships to fit a mathematical model estimating the probability of graduation. Once an estimate of each student's probability of graduation is calculated, this information can be used to project how many students "should" have graduated at a particular campus (see Table 5.3). Summing probabilities across students within the institution represents the expected number of graduates for that campus if it was performing at the average for the institutions used to establish the model. Up to this point, students have been grouped on a set of incoming demographic characteristics, and the probability of graduation has been

### Table 5.3. Ratio of Actual to Expected Graduates and Percentage of Graduates by Category

| | | | | Gender | | | | | |
|---|---|---|---|---|---|---|---|---|---|
| | Total | | | Women | | | Men | | |
| | Actual | Expected | Ratio | Actual | Expected | Ratio | Actual | Expected | Ratio |
| College A | | | | | | | | | |
| Graduates | 508 | 552 | 0.92 | 271 | 296 | 0.92 | 237 | 256 | 0.93 |
| Percentage Graduates | 36.4 | 39.6 | | 36.4 | 39.7 | | 36.5 | 39.4 | |
| College B | | | | | | | | | |
| Graduates | 280 | 281 | 1.00 | 149 | 151 | 0.99 | 131 | 130 | 1.01 |
| Percentage Graduates | 36.6 | 36.7 | | 35.5 | 36 | | 37.9 | 37.6 | |
| College C | | | | | | | | | |
| Graduates | 316 | 271 | 1.17 | 178 | 151 | 1.18 | 138 | 120 | 1.15 |
| Percentage Graduates | 35.4 | 30.5 | | 36.3 | 30.8 | | 34.3 | 29.9 | |
| Total | | | | | | | | | |
| Graduates | 1,104 | 1,104 | 1.00 | 598 | 598 | 1.00 | 506 | 506 | 1.00 |
| Percentage Graduates | 36.2 | 36.2 | | 36.1 | 36.1 | | 36.2 | 36.2 | |

based on the percentage of each group that graduated. When there is an interest in using many student characteristics, the overwhelming number of cells precludes using the probabilities based on the groups. Obviously this forces us to look for an alternative methodology. Logistic regression provides an excellent solution to the problem.

**Logistic Regression Model.** Logistic regression fits a curvilinear response function that relates one or more independent variables to a binary dependent variable. In the current analysis, college graduation would be cast as a dichotomous variable and coded as 1 = Graduate and 0 = Did Not Graduate. Using logistic regression, the estimated probability of graduation for individuals at College $j$ given a set of $k$ traits becomes:

$$p_{ij} = \frac{\exp(\beta_0 + \beta_1 X_{1i} + \ldots + \beta_k X_{ki})}{1 + \exp(\beta_0 + \beta_1 X_{1i} + \ldots + \beta_k X_{ki})}$$

From this we can calculate the expected number of graduates for Institution $j$ by summing the individual probabilities for those students:

$$E_j = \sum_{i=1}^{nj} p_i.$$

Logistic regression permits the estimation of a probability for every combination of variables used to establish the model. These estimates are not simply mathematical abstractions; rather, they are based on the actual performance of students who hold the same and similar combinations of

| | High School Average | | | | | | | | |
| | Over 90 | | | 80–90 | | | Below 80 | | |
| | Actual | Expected | Ratio | Actual | Expected | Ratio | Actual | Expected | Ratio |
|---|---|---|---|---|---|---|---|---|---|
| College A | | | | | | | | | |
| Graduates | 179 | 192 | 0.93 | 326 | 355 | 0.92 | 3 | 4 | 0.75 |
| Percentage Graduates | 41.9 | 44.9 | | 34.3 | 37.4 | | 17.6 | 25.9 | |
| College B | | | | | | | | | |
| Graduates | 56 | 49 | 1.14 | 188 | 203 | 0.93 | 36 | 29 | 1.24 |
| Percentage Graduates | 51.4 | 44.9 | | 34.5 | 37.2 | | 32.1 | 26.2 | |
| College C | | | | | | | | | |
| Graduates | 38 | 32 | 1.19 | 232 | 188 | 1.23 | 46 | 51 | 0.90 |
| Percentage Graduates | 52.8 | 44.9 | | 45.6 | 36.9 | | 14.8 | 16.5 | |
| Total | | | | | | | | | |
| Graduates | 273 | 273 | 1.00 | 746 | 746 | 1.00 | 85 | 84 | 1.01 |
| Percentage Graduates | 44.9 | 44.9 | | 37.2 | 37.2 | | 19.3 | 19.3 | |

characteristics. For example, if we were interested in the graduation probability of a twenty-year-old white male with a family income of $35,000, a high school average of 85, and a high school rank in the top 20 percent of his class, these values could be inserted into the logistic regression equation, and a predicted probability could be derived. This predicted probability would be based on the actual and observed performance of the previously defined group (twenty-year-old white male, and so forth). The behavior of similar groups (for example, twenty-one-year-old white males, income of $33,000, high school average 85) also influences the result by virtue of their proximity both logically and mathematically.

In the SUNY studies, the size of the analytic populations is reasonably large—generally over twenty thousand students—which ensures that reasonably good coverage is available across the range of possible values. Statistical analyses are always better when the sample size is large, but logistic regression analysis is especially sensitive if the analysis is based on too few observations. Fortunately, the reasonableness of the results can be checked by comparing the predicted probability with the actual performance of the group. Both are available because a group can be defined based on any combination of characteristics included in the model. To examine the proximity of the predicted result to the actual value, calculate the average probability estimated by the logistic regression model with the simple proportion (probability) who actually graduated, and compare these two results. Ideally, these two results will be very similar, and empirical evidence at SUNY has borne this out. An observer might suggest that if the actual probabilities are available, there should be no reason to bother with estimation procedures. Given a large number of variables, it would be practically impossible to calculate every possible combination. Even if it were possible, it would be incredibly tedious, and the results would vary little from current practice. It is also important to note that the notion "college of enrollment" is not introduced until after all of the estimated probabilities have been calculated. Functionally, the procedure is not related to the actual colleges involved, and this removes the specter of any imposed effects that might be introduced if the institutions were coded or separately identified in any way.

**Application in the SUNY System.** Both of the suggested approaches require a rather extensive and detailed database containing individual student records. This almost certainly limits its practical application to large public university systems that have multiple institutions similar enough to warrant comparison. It is unlikely that a collection of institutions not under a system banner would band together to share or pool the information required to carry out such a large-scale analysis. Further, there is the requirement that the system office have the informational resources to undertake such a massive and detailed study. At a minimum, a system must have an existing systemwide database that contains all of the demographic and academic indexes used in the analysis. This database would have to be updated every semester to permit the development of a comprehensive retention profile for each student. It would also require a systemwide degree file indicating all of the individual students who were granted a degree over a series of academic years. Once these informational resources were in place for a sufficient period of time (say, four to six years), the system would then be in a position to develop a systemwide normative model that can be used to estimate each student's probability of graduation (or retention). Once these probabilities are available, it is relatively easy to calculate expected rates of graduation or retention by summing the calculated probabilities across all students enrolled in a cohort on that campus.

SUNY has all of the requisite databases in place to establish such a systemwide model of student retention and graduation. SUNY has been generating such comparative values for a number of years and has found the exercise to be quite informative. To demonstrate how integrated information about actual performance versus modeled (expected) performance might be used, a simulated university system comprising eight institutions has been developed. Actual and modeled data have been generated for each of these institutions to illustrate how one might tabulate results and develop reports for comparative purposes.

Table 5.4 traces the enrollment and graduation patterns of six full-time freshmen cohorts entering in a fall term. The status of each student is evaluated for every fall term subsequent to the term of initial enrollment, and this information is used to model the probabilities that drive this analysis. Until now, the discussion has focused exclusively on graduation rates. Retention patterns can also be modeled just as easily as those related to graduation (see Table 5.4).

Like graduation, retention can be evaluated at a particular point in time and coded as a dichotomous variable, for example, 1 = enrolled, 0 = otherwise. Regressing student trait variables on retention allows the development of a model of expected retention rates by institution. With either graduation or retention, comparing the expected number with what actually happened provides a viable, realistic, meaningful mechanism for measuring institutional performance. The ratio of actual to expected is an easy index to understand and communicates to policymakers and the public alike: 1.00 is average, above 1.00 is superior, and below 1.00 is subpar. Looking at Table 5.4, it is interesting and heartening to note the general consistency and stability of results within institutions over time. This consistency is reflected across the different fall cohorts and as they are followed from semester to semester. Although Table 5.4 is a contrived example, it was purposefully constructed to reflect the general patterns found in actual practice in the SUNY system.

**Results of the Logistic Model.** To illustrate the results derived, the institutions were ranked on overall performance and rated from 1 to 8, with College 1 producing the best results. For each cohort-term combination, Table 5.4 shows four numbers: the first two columns are the number of actual and expected (modeled) persisters or graduates; these results are followed by the previously mentioned ratio, with the last column showing the actual percentage of graduation or persistence. (To abbreviate the display, third-year retention data were suppressed; normally these columns are included.) In an actual application and examination, the primary interest would be on specific institutional findings.

Obviously there is an interest in determining why institutions ranked at the top fared well, so those conditions could be replicated elsewhere. Conversely, the causes of poor performance need to be understood, so that these problems could be addressed and corrected. Since the data displayed in Table 5.4 do not represent real institutions, it is difficult, if not impossible, to probe causes of good or bad performance or recommend remedial action. There are some performance patterns in Table 5.4 that warrant discussion, however. Among these is the influence of the length of time to degree. If time to degree is extended from four years to five years, and eventually to six years, we find that with each additional year, institutional performance begins to converge; that is, the ratios begin to approach 1.00. Again this pattern reflects reality and suggests from our efforts at SUNY that after adjusting for student characteristics, the biggest difference between institutions is the amount of time it takes to get a degree rather than the sheer volume of degrees. This would suggest that institutions with low four-year graduation rates should not look solely at causes of student attrition, but should also look at other aspects of their institutional environment that impede academic progress, such as course availability or breakdowns in the academic advisement process.

Another general finding is that institutional retention and graduation patterns are established early in the life cycle of an entering cohort. This is

**Table 5.4. Actual and Modeled Retention and Graduation Rates for Full-Time, First-Time Students Enrolled in a Baccalaureate Degree Program, Selected Colleges**

| Institution and Year | Initial Cohort | Second Year | | | | Fourth Year | | | |
|---|---|---|---|---|---|---|---|---|---|
| | | Actual | Modeled | Ratio | Percentage Returning | Actual | Modeled | Ratio | Percentage Returning |
| College 1 | | | | | | | | | |
| 1988 | 1,493 | 1,414 | 1,327 | 1.07 | 94.7 | 1,296 | 1,157 | 1.12 | 86.8 |
| 1989 | 1,560 | 1,465 | 1,396 | 1.05 | 93.9 | 1,330 | 1,211 | 1.10 | 85.3 |
| 1990 | 1,393 | 1,310 | 1,255 | 1.04 | 94.0 | 1,174 | 1,089 | 1.08 | 84.3 |
| 1991 | 1,439 | 1,340 | 1,299 | 1.03 | 93.1 | 1,176 | 1,102 | 1.07 | 81.7 |
| 1992 | 1,512 | 1,402 | 1,338 | 1.05 | 92.7 | | | | |
| 1993 | 1,578 | 1,480 | 1,414 | 1.05 | 93.8 | | | | |
| College 2 | | | | | | | | | |
| 1988 | 895 | 757 | 730 | 1.04 | 84.6 | 617 | 595 | 1.04 | 68.9 |
| 1989 | 944 | 811 | 789 | 1.03 | 85.9 | 665 | 633 | 1.05 | 70.4 |
| 1990 | 841 | 731 | 718 | 1.02 | 86.9 | 620 | 585 | 1.06 | 73.7 |
| 1991 | 760 | 661 | 644 | 1.03 | 87.0 | 515 | 509 | 1.01 | 67.8 |
| 1992 | 835 | 727 | 700 | 1.04 | 87.1 | | | | |
| 1993 | 767 | 643 | 634 | 1.01 | 83.8 | | | | |
| College 3 | | | | | | | | | |
| 1988 | 1,977 | 1,751 | 1,682 | 1.04 | 88.6 | 1,429 | 1,398 | 1.02 | 72.3 |
| 1989 | 2,005 | 1,833 | 1,735 | 1.06 | 91.4 | 1,490 | 1,422 | 1.05 | 74.3 |
| 1990 | 1,686 | 1,531 | 1,477 | 1.04 | 90.8 | 1,289 | 1,236 | 1.04 | 76.5 |
| 1991 | 1,957 | 1,759 | 1,700 | 1.03 | 89.9 | 1,425 | 1,369 | 1.04 | 72.8 |
| 1992 | 1,906 | 1,682 | 1,631 | 1.03 | 88.2 | | | | |
| 1993 | 1,790 | 1,580 | 1,522 | 1.04 | 88.3 | | | | |
| College 4 | | | | | | | | | |
| 1988 | 1,220 | 1,008 | 1,001 | 1.01 | 82.6 | 825 | 815 | 1.01 | 67.6 |
| 1989 | 1,463 | 1,214 | 1,232 | 0.99 | 83.0 | 999 | 990 | 1.01 | 68.3 |
| 1990 | 1,151 | 986 | 979 | 1.01 | 85.7 | 796 | 795 | 1.00 | 69.2 |
| 1991 | 1,310 | 1,129 | 1,114 | 1.01 | 86.2 | 928 | 886 | 1.05 | 70.8 |
| 1992 | 1,240 | 1,030 | 1,036 | 0.99 | 83.1 | | | | |
| 1993 | 1,050 | 874 | 868 | 1.01 | 83.2 | | | | |
| College 5 | | | | | | | | | |
| 1988 | 1,237 | 905 | 979 | 0.92 | 73.2 | 712 | 779 | 0.91 | 57.6 |
| 1989 | 1,224 | 964 | 1,001 | 0.96 | 78.8 | 742 | 787 | 0.94 | 60.6 |
| 1990 | 1,022 | 795 | 855 | 0.93 | 77.8 | 620 | 682 | 0.91 | 60.7 |
| 1991 | 990 | 761 | 815 | 0.93 | 76.9 | 593 | 625 | 0.95 | 59.9 |
| 1992 | 958 | 734 | 781 | 0.94 | 76.6 | | | | |
| 1993 | 969 | 733 | 781 | 0.94 | 75.6 | | | | |
| College 6 | | | | | | | | | |
| 1988 | 668 | 539 | 532 | 1.01 | 80.7 | 430 | 413 | 1.04 | 64.4 |
| 1989 | 744 | 591 | 608 | 0.97 | 79.4 | 444 | 472 | 0.94 | 59.7 |
| 1990 | 685 | 577 | 574 | 1.01 | 84.2 | 466 | 454 | 1.03 | 68.0 |
| 1991 | 645 | 519 | 539 | 0.96 | 80.5 | 390 | 418 | 0.93 | 60.5 |
| 1992 | 597 | 459 | 487 | 0.94 | 76.9 | | | | |
| 1993 | 530 | 414 | 433 | 0.96 | 78.1 | | | | |
| College 7 | | | | | | | | | |
| 1988 | 424 | 296 | 333 | 0.89 | 69.8 | 199 | 260 | 0.77 | 46.9 |
| 1989 | 398 | 265 | 322 | 0.82 | 66.6 | 181 | 247 | 0.73 | 45.5 |
| 1990 | 352 | 260 | 288 | 0.90 | 73.9 | 174 | 221 | 0.79 | 49.4 |
| 1991 | 309 | 237 | 254 | 0.93 | 76.7 | 153 | 193 | 0.79 | 49.5 |
| 1992 | 294 | 217 | 234 | 0.93 | 73.8 | | | | |
| 1993 | 280 | 201 | 222 | 0.91 | 71.8 | | | | |
| College 8 | | | | | | | | | |
| 1988 | 1,414 | 1,025 | 1,111 | 0.92 | 72.5 | 770 | 862 | 0.89 | 54.5 |
| 1989 | 1,425 | 1,084 | 1,143 | 0.95 | 76.1 | 788 | 878 | 0.90 | 55.3 |
| 1990 | 1,380 | 1,078 | 1,123 | 0.96 | 78.1 | 785 | 861 | 0.91 | 56.9 |
| 1991 | 1,280 | 981 | 1,022 | 0.96 | 76.6 | 687 | 766 | 0.90 | 53.7 |
| 1992 | 1,200 | 925 | 968 | 0.96 | 77.1 | | | | |
| 1993 | 932 | 691 | 742 | 0.93 | 74.1 | | | | |

| | | | | Received Degree Within: | | | | | | | |
|---|---|---|---|---|---|---|---|---|---|---|---|
| Four Years | | | | Five Years | | | | Six Years | | | |
| Actual | Modeled | Ratio | Percentage Returning | Actual | Modeled | Ratio | Percentage Returning | Actual | Modeled | Ratio | Percentage Returning |
| 1,050 | 880 | 1.19 | 70.3 | 1,211 | 1,067 | 1.13 | 81.1 | 1,236 | 1,097 | 1.13 | 82.8 |
| 1,027 | 908 | 1.13 | 65.8 | 1,213 | 1,105 | 1.10 | 77.8 | | | | |
| 924 | 821 | 1.13 | 66.3 | | | | | | | | |
| 388 | 359 | 1.08 | 43.4 | 535 | 502 | 1.07 | 59.8 | 568 | 527 | 1.08 | 63.5 |
| 432 | 374 | 1.16 | 45.8 | 591 | 536 | 1.10 | 62.6 | | | | |
| 424 | 371 | 1.14 | 50.4 | | | | | | | | |
| 1,070 | 938 | 1.14 | 54.1 | 1,284 | 1,217 | 1.06 | 64.9 | 1,321 | 1,272 | 1.04 | 66.8 |
| 1,048 | 924 | 1.13 | 52.3 | 1,294 | 1,225 | 1.06 | 64.5 | | | | |
| 891 | 813 | 1.10 | 52.8 | | | | | | | | |
| 496 | 502 | 0.99 | 40.7 | 703 | 690 | 1.02 | 57.6 | 724 | 724 | 1.00 | 59.3 |
| 631 | 596 | 1.06 | 43.1 | 859 | 840 | 1.02 | 58.7 | | | | |
| 524 | 498 | 1.05 | 45.5 | | | | | | | | |
| 381 | 439 | 0.87 | 30.8 | 605 | 641 | 0.94 | 48.9 | 640 | 681 | 0.94 | 51.7 |
| 416 | 450 | 0.92 | 34.0 | 654 | 659 | 0.99 | 53.4 | | | | |
| 373 | 415 | 0.90 | 36.5 | | | | | | | | |
| 170 | 220 | 0.77 | 25.4 | 308 | 327 | 0.94 | 46.1 | 343 | 352 | 0.97 | 51.3 |
| 180 | 243 | 0.74 | 24.2 | 338 | 375 | 0.90 | 45.4 | | | | |
| 218 | 259 | 0.84 | 31.8 | | | | | | | | |
| 109 | 143 | 0.76 | 25.7 | 158 | 207 | 0.76 | 37.3 | 171 | 222 | 0.77 | 40.3 |
| 95 | 133 | 0.71 | 23.9 | 126 | 197 | 0.64 | 31.7 | | | | |
| 103 | 127 | 0.81 | 29.3 | | | | | | | | |
| 261 | 445 | 0.59 | 18.5 | 525 | 678 | 0.77 | 37.1 | 600 | 729 | 0.82 | 42.4 |
| 243 | 444 | 0.55 | 17.1 | 557 | 695 | 0.80 | 39.1 | | | | |
| 290 | 444 | 0.65 | 21.0 | | | | | | | | |

not surprising, given the current literature on student and particularly fresh-man persistence, but it is noteworthy nevertheless. Looking at second-year ratios and comparing these to later patterns indicates that by the beginning of the second year (and probably sooner), a good idea of general institu-tional performance is manifest. This finding supports another conclusion: the institutional factors that influence attrition are endemic and pervasive and begin affecting student behavior virtually the minute they first set foot on campus.

Yet another pattern deserves comment: the impact of being a student in a highly selective institution. Within SUNY, students at the most selec-tive institutions tend to exceed performance expectations. To speculate on why this occurs, it could be that academic distinctions among students are lost or at least blurred once students enroll. In other words, one cannot dis-tinguish a "good student" from a "poor" one simply by their appearance. Since selective institutions have a predominance of very able students, this produces an increased level of expectation on the part of faculty and staff, and their expectations are imposed on all students regardless of individuals' prior academic history. Not only are their expectations imposed, but the stu-dents tend to respond and behave as the faculty expected in a kind of self-fulfilling prophecy. This suggests that some institutions would do better if they created an environment that engendered greater respect for students, treated the students as academically capable, and held them to high stan-dards. Along with this strategy, another possible influence or positive effect would be to ensure that the less able students are exposed to and interact with better students on a regular basis. This integration of abilities positively influences their study habits, their approach to problems, the way they think, and eventually the amount that they learn. In effect, the less able stu-dents learn to learn primarily from their more academically robust student colleagues.

Looking at four-year graduation rates in Table 5.4, the institution with the best actual percentage rates also has the highest ratio: 1:19. This mea-sure indicates that College 1 graduated 19 percent more students than the model would have predicted given the characteristics of its students who enrolled in the fall 1991 cohort. Although College 1 had the best overall performance, in some ways, the performance of College 2 is a bit more intriguing. College 2's actual graduation rates are very ordinary or average when compared to the other institutions in the example; the actual four-year rates are around 45 percent. The actual-to-expected ratios, however, indicate that College 2 is at or next to the top in virtually every category. The mediocre actuals combined with high ratios suggest that students at College 2 began with less academic potential than students at either College 1 or College 3, but something (ostensibly, some aspect of the institution's operations) caused them to outperform, consistently and significantly, what might otherwise be expected. College 2 would be a good one to study in depth to see if there are any obvious, or simply plausible, explanations that could be copied, tried, and tested at other institutions. Although Colleges 1 and 3 are also doing comparably well, it is very likely that more would be learned about positive organizational practices from College 2 than any of the other seven, at least if taken individually. Conversely, College 8 would be worth investigating in depth to determine if any particular problem practices could be uncovered. Retention of College 8 students into the fourth year is low, but not exceptionally so—about 90 percent of the modeled cohort. This result indicates that there should have been plenty of students in position to graduate, but the actual four-year graduation ratio was only around 55 percent. Thus, a closer look at the institutional environment at College 8 might indicate some of the things an institution ought not do.

Researchers have to be cautious when making value judgments about institutions that over- or underperform the modeled value and not rush to judgment. For example, there may be a legitimate explanation for an institution's performing at other than the modeled rate. If it serves a student population that has characteristics that are not adequately adjusted for by the model, then that institution may appear to be doing better or worse than it is in fact. Remember that the norms are established across all of the institutions in the study, and if one institution is very different in character from the others on dimensions that are related to student retention and relevant measures are not included as predictors, then the estimated values may not represent a realistic assessment of expected results for that college. For example, if an institution is primarily a commuter campus, which serves a nontraditional clientele who are more likely to be working twenty or more hours per week, have dependent children, or have other conditions that impede academic progress, and these conditions are not directly or accurately reflected in the model, then the calculated rate may hold such a campus to too high a standard or an invalid standard. This issue is of particular concern if performance funding is tied to the analysis, because the invalid results may be making a difficult institutional environment even worse. When evaluating specific institutional performance, there has to be some implicit recognition of those intervening factors that have not been properly incorporated into the expected values—either because measures did not exist or because they were overlooked when developing the model.

Along with the aggregate analysis (shown in Table 5.4), there are other analyses that would provide more detailed and perhaps more useful indexes of institutional performance. One of these is a campus-by-campus analysis of the differences between the actual and expected frequencies. In effect, it would be comparable to an expansion of the analysis shown for Table 5.2. Comparing expected values with what actually happened provides some insight and focus on the specific student subgroups that flourish in the environment offered by the college or, conversely, indicate groups that tend to have problems and may need some specific attention. Such expected frequencies place aberrant student behavior in a unique context and provide a benchmark against which other performance can be measured. Without this benchmark, an individual campus can only guess whether the behavior of a particular population at that campus is normal or exceptional in some way. As a result, this use of expected frequencies provides an institutional profile that could potentially help direct admissions and recruitment efforts, or possibly indicate administrative or instructional areas that need attention or change.

For a particular institution, determining the specific groups that flounder or flourish provides a unique institutional fingerprint that represents the interplay of student characteristics and college environment. Studying the shape of these interactions builds an awareness of the impact that the institution is having on diverse student groups. This knowledge must eventually benefit both the student and the institution. Another useful by-product of such an analysis is the identification of high-risk students. Once identified, these students could be monitored, and, if necessary, intervention could occur prior to a decision to drop out, stop out, or transfer.

**Implications for Student Retention Studies.** This application of logistic regression to the estimation of expected retention and graduation rates puts these concepts in a new context, but it does not directly address the fundamental issues related to the underlying causes of attrition or poor graduation rates. It does, however, establish an opportunity for better inquiries into the causes of student attrition by providing a piece of information that has heretofore been missing. That is, it offers a way of classifying and characterizing the relative performance of institutions on this dimension. If this new information can be integrated into an in-depth assessment of the impact of specific institutional practices on cohort survival, it should help uncover the interrelationships that directly or indirectly influence student behavior. Eventually it should contribute to our understanding of why one institution does well and another does poorly, or why a particular type of student seems to thrive in one environment but not another.

## References

Pascarella, E., and Terenzini, P. *How College Affects Students.* San Francisco: Jossey-Bass, 1991.

*GARY BLOSE is acting director of institutional research and senior research associate in the Academic Planning Policy and Evaluation Office at System Administration, State University of New York.*

**6**

*The need for developmental education is not new, and it likely will not be ending soon. Perhaps the best way to deal with the problem is to apply the most promising means, based on the research, for receiving maximum benefit from these programs. The authors provide a list of such exemplary practices for developmental education.*

# Developmental and Remedial Education in Postsecondary Education

*Hunter R. Boylan, Barbara S. Bonham, Stephen R. White*

Practically every college and university in the United States provides some sort of service for students who are not quite ready to take a particular course, pass a particular test, or enroll in a particular major. These services may range from informal tutoring activities to highly formal and comprehensive programs featuring diagnosis and assessment, advising, remedial courses, individualized instruction, and tutoring. These services have existed in one form or another since the earliest days of higher education in the United States (Maxwell, 1997).

Since the 1960s, however, the trend has been to establish formal organizational structures for the provision of these services. The two most common organizational structures are the learning assistance center and the developmental education program (Casazza and Silverman, 1996). Learning centers typically provide some combination of individualized instruction, tutoring, and short-term workshops on such topics as study skills or test taking. Developmental education programs typically provide courses and learning laboratories. Both may offer diagnostic and assessment testing or provide academic advising, and there is often some overlap in both the students served and the services provided by learning centers and developmental education programs.

Among professionals in the field, the overarching term for these services is *developmental education*. This term reflects an emphasis on the holistic development of the individual student and is rooted in developmental psychology. Professionals in developmental education assess student needs and make some judgment as to the type and duration of intervention needed in order to help students accomplish their academic goals. They recognize that students must develop both their personal and academic skills in order to be effective learners (Bloom, 1976). Consequently the interventions of professional developmental educators are usually comprehensive, combining instructional activities with diagnostic, advising, and counseling activities.

Nevertheless, the intervention used most commonly in developmental education is the remedial course. This is because a structured course provides the most efficient means of conveying information to a large number of students at the same time. A remedial course is usually a regularly scheduled courses lasting a full academic term. The content is typically at a somewhat lower level than that of the regular curriculum course. Consequently, these courses are usually assigned a course number below 100, frequently in the 090 to 099 range. The most common remedial courses are in English, mathematics, and reading (National Center for Education Statistics, 1996).

According to the National Center for Education Statistics (1996), remedial courses are found in about 75 percent of the nation's universities and nearly 100 percent of its community colleges. The widespread use of remedial courses to assist students assessed as having some academic deficiency has led to confusion of the terms *developmental* and *remedial*. The term *remedial* refers exclusively to courses generally considered to be precollege level.

Developmental courses are usually considered to be college level but with a focus on academic development such as study strategies, critical thinking, or the freshman experience rather than a particular content area. Exceptions are sometimes found in mathematics and college writing, where the course content is clearly beyond high school but the course is considered developmental because it is designed to fill the gaps between high school preparation and college expectations. For instance, the freshman writing course that so many students suffered through in the 1950s, 1960s, and 1970s was actually a developmental course. It was designed to develop writing skills to the point where students could succeed in later college courses.

Developmental education, on the other hand, refers to a continuum of services ranging from remedial courses at the low end to tutoring or learning assistance centers at the high end. Developmental education is something of an umbrella under which a variety of interventions designed to develop the diverse talents of students may fit (Cross, 1976). Developmental education is the whole of which remediation on the one end and learning assistance on the other end are both a part.

This chapter explores the continuum of developmental education services with an emphasis on courses. Throughout this chapter, the term *developmental* is used to describe any structured class falling within the spectrum of developmental education. These range from basic arithmetic courses carrying no credit to learning and study strategies courses carrying regular and transferable college credit.

## Research on Developmental Education

It is only since the years following World War II that a body of research has been developed on the twin topics of developmental and remedial education. Only now has a clear picture begun to emerge about the characteristics of the developmental and remedial student.

**The Developmental Education Student.** Contrary to popular opinion, the majority of those enrolled in developmental courses and services are white. Results from the National Study of Developmental Education (Boylan, Bonham, and Bliss, 1994) indicated that about two-thirds of students participating in developmental education were white and one-third were minorities, with the largest minority groups in developmental education being African American and Hispanic. An American Council on Education study (Knopp, 1996) reported that about one-fifth of those taking developmental courses were minorities. Women and men are about equally represented in developmental education at both community colleges and universities (Boylan, Bonham, and Bliss, 1994; Knopp, 1996). Knopp (1996) reported that the majority of those enrolled in developmental courses were adults. Breneman and Haarlow (1998) reported similar findings. The majority of developmental students, particularly those at community colleges, have at least part-time jobs and occupy a variety of adult roles, such as parents, workers, and voters.

Hardin (1998) has developed a useful seven-category typology for describing the characteristics of developmental students on the basis of their reasons for being placed in developmental courses:

*The poor chooser*—those who have made poor academic decisions that have adversely affected their academic future, such as not taking a full battery of college preparatory courses in high school

*The adult student*—those over twenty-five years old who have been out of school for several years and must cope with managing adult roles and responsibilities while adjusting to college-level academic expectations

*The student with a disability*—those who suffer from physical or learning disabilities that prevent them from performing as well in the present as nondisabled students and have often kept them from learning as much as other students in the past

*The ignored*—those whose physical or psychological disabilities or other learning problems have gone undiagnosed or whose learning needs have consistently been ignored in prior schooling

*The limited English proficiency student*—those who acquired their early schooling in foreign countries and, as a consequence, have limited English language and verbal skills to apply to college-level settings

*The user*—those who attend college simply to attain the benefits thereof and who often have no clear academic goals, objectives, or purposes

*The extreme case*—those who have severe emotional, psychological, or social problems that have prevented them from being successful in academic situations in the past and continue to do so in the present

This typology has the advantage of emphasizing the diverse reasons that students must take developmental courses. As Hardin (1998) points out, it is fallacious to assume that those in developmental courses are "18-year-olds who slept through high school and now want a second chance to learn at taxpayer's expense" (p. 15). In fact, they represent a wide range of American adults.

**Developmental Education Best Practices.** In serving developmental students, professional developmental educators have the advantage of almost thirty years of research to guide their practice. This research has identified a variety of policies and practices associated with student success in developmental education. Most of them have been advocated by developmental education experts for many years and are relatively inexpensive. As Chuck Claxton has pointed out (1994), "Bad developmental education costs about as much as good developmental education."

*Best Policies.* Promising policies that campuses should employ are as follows:

*Implement mandatory assessment and placement* (Morante, 1989; Roueche and Roueche, 1999). Developmental programs are most effective on campuses where assessment of incoming students is mandatory and students are required to enroll in the courses indicated by this assessment. Without a linkage between mandatory assessment and placement, there is no way of identifying students who need to enroll in developmental courses or any means of ensuring that those who need developmental education actually participate in it.

*Promote an institutional commitment to developmental education* (Boylan and Saxon, 1998; Kiemig, 1983). Developmental programs are most effective on campuses where there is an institution-wide commitment to the success of underprepared students. Such a commitment helps students, faculty, and staff understand the importance of developmental education activities and makes it more likely that all those who work with developmental students will be following the same agenda and working toward the same goals and objectives.

*Provide a comprehensive approach to developmental education courses and services* (Donovan, 1974; Kulik, Kulik, and Schwalb, 1983). Developmental programs are most effective when they include a wide variety of courses and academic support services such as tutoring, advising, laboratories, and learning assistance centers. Developmental students bring with them a variety of learning needs and styles. A comprehensive approach to support services enables institutions to respond effectively to this diversity of student needs and styles.

*Establish a series of ongoing orientation courses and activities* (Nelson, 1998; Upcraft and Gardner, 1989). Developmental programs are most effective when they are combined with ongoing orientation activities such as pre-college orientation followed by freshman seminars or student success courses. Developmental students are most likely to be among those who are first-generation college students. As such, they bring less knowledge of academic procedures and expectations than most other students (Sedlacek, 1987). Ongoing orientation activities help to fill this knowledge gap.

*Enforce strict attendance policies for developmental courses* (Boylan and Bonham, 1999; McMullin and Young, 1994). Developmental students require as much instructional time as possible. If attendance policies are inconsistent or are enforced erratically, it becomes easy for developmental students to believe they can miss classes with impunity. Developmental students cannot strengthen their skills if they miss classes, and they should not be given the impression that they can do so without consequences.

*Abolish late registration for developmental students* (Roueche and Roueche, 1993; Roueche and Roueche, 1999). Developmental students are among those who can least afford to enter a class in the second or third week of the term, let alone the fourth or the fifth. It is absolutely erroneous to believe that any significant number of developmental students can enroll in a course after the first week of the semester and have any reasonable hope of succeeding. The availability of late registration options encourages them to believe this is possible. Simply stated, they should not be encouraged in this belief by institutional late registration policies.

*Best Practices.* Promising practices that campuses should employ are as follows:

*Provide a centralized structure for developmental education courses and services* (Boylan, Bonham, Claxton, and Bliss, 1992; Roueche and Snow, 1977). Developmental education courses and services require coordination and communication in order to be effective. This is best provided within the context of a centralized developmental program. If it is unrealistic to centralize developmental courses and services, then these activities should at least be well coordinated by a full-time administrator, and all those who work with developmental students should have opportunities to meet together, share problems, and develop solutions as a group.

*Encourage professional development for those who work with developmental students* (Boylan, Bliss, and Bonham, 1997; Casazza and Silverman, 1996). Successful developmental education efforts are delivered by those who are well aware of the nature and needs of developmental students and the techniques that contribute to their learning. It should come as no surprise that those who are well trained in what they do are able to do it better. Consequently, regular opportunities should be provided for developmental educators to develop their skills through on-campus workshops and participation in graduate programs, conferences, and institutes.

*Implement classroom assessment techniques in developmental courses* (Angelo and Cross, 1991; Boylan and Bonham, 1999). Classroom assessment techniques (CATs) are activities that enable instructors to receive feedback regarding student learning and also encourage greater student involvement in the classroom. Both of these features are known to be a valuable aid for developmental instructors to improve their teaching and developmental students to improve their learning (Boylan, Bonham, Claxton, and Bliss, 1992). Although the use of CATs is a relatively new development, substantial research supports their effectiveness when used with developmental students.

*Engage in regular and systematic program evaluation* (Boylan, Bliss, and Bonham, 1997; Maxwell, 1997). Engaging in regular formative and summative evaluation of program activities has consistently been shown to be associated with program success. Knowledge of program outcomes such as course completion rates, grades in developmental courses, and grades in follow-up curriculum courses is essential to revision and improving programs. This is particularly true where the results of formative evaluation are shared with staff and used for program improvement purposes.

*Focus on the development of metacognitive skills* (Starks, 1994; Weinstein and others, 1998). Learning to monitor comprehension and applying new learning strategies to improve comprehension is particularly important for developmental students, many of whom have not learned to do this in the past. These are essential skills in which developmental students are frequently underprepared. Programs and courses emphasizing these skills are more effective than programs that ignore them.

*Give frequent tests in developmental courses* (Boylan, Bonham, Claxton, and Bliss, 1992; Cross, 1976). Developmental students need the opportunity to practice their skills and receive frequent feedback on their skill mastery. These students are more successful in courses where opportunities are provided through frequent testing. Frequent testing provides both necessary feedback for learning and valuable practice opportunities for students to demonstrate newly learned skills.

*Use a theory-based approach to teaching developmental courses* (Casazza and Silverman, 1996; Stahl, Simpson, and Hayes, 1992). College faculty frequently teach according to the way they were taught as opposed to using sound learning theory as a basis for the design and delivery of instruction. Although this may work for well-prepared students, it is usually not effective for developmental students unless the teacher is truly gifted. Theory-based instruction provides grounding for instructors as well as students and is more likely to be successful with weaker students.

*Integrate classroom, learning assistance, and laboratory activities* (Kiemig, 1983; Boylan, Bliss, and Bonham, 1997). Although learning laboratories are frequently encountered in postsecondary education, they are usually not well integrated with instructional activities. For learning laboratories to be most effective, their activities must represent collaboration between laboratory personnel and the instructors of the courses these laboratories are designed to serve. The full integration of laboratory and classroom activities frequently provides synergistic benefits for both.

**Developmental Education Outcomes.** Evidence suggests that passing developmental courses is related to higher grades and increased student retention. The National Study of Developmental Education (Boylan, Bonham, Claxton, and Bliss, 1992) found that passing early developmental courses was related to higher student grade point averages and that students who passed developmental courses were more likely to pass their first curriculum course in the same or a related subject. They were also more likely to be retained than students who did not participate in developmental education (Boylan, Bonham, Claxton, and Bliss, 1992).

A 1996 study reviewed the records of over twenty thousand students taking developmental courses in Minnesota community colleges (Minnesota State Colleges and Universities, 1996). The study reported that students who had passed one or more developmental courses obtained higher credit-to-course ratios, received higher grades, and were more likely to be retained than students who had not placed into developmental courses.

A recent study of developmental education in Texas colleges and universities indicated that those who passed developmental courses were much more likely to be retained for one year than those who failed these courses. At universities, for instance, 66.4 percent of those who passed their first developmental course were still in school one year later, but only 9.6 percent of those who failed their first developmental course were still in school one year later (Boylan and Saxon, 1998).

Using data from the U.S. Department of Education, Adelman (1996) found that developmental education outcomes were best for students who needed the fewest developmental courses. Students who placed into only one developmental course were much more likely to graduate than students who placed into two or more developmental courses. Adelman also found that those who placed into both developmental English and reading faced the highest risk of attrition.

Although the general evidence indicates that developmental education contributes to the success of college students, there is considerable variation in the outcomes of developmental education activities across the country. A recent study of developmental education in Texas provides a good example. Using postdevelopmental education pass rates on a statewide assessment test as a measure, Boylan and Saxon (1998) found tremendous variation in outcomes among both community colleges and universities. Among community colleges, postdevelopmental education pass rates ranged from below 25 percent to over 90 percent. Among universities, they ranged from 30 percent to nearly 100 percent.

When these data are aggregated, however, postdevelopmental education pass rates at community colleges averaged 45.4 percent in reading, 55.0 percent in English, and 33.4 percent in mathematics. At universities, these averages were 75.9 percent in reading, 85.4 percent in English, and 65.4 percent in mathematics (Boylan and Saxon, 1998).

In another section of the same study, the outcomes of institutions using many of the best practices noted earlier in this chapter were considerably better than those using few of these practices (Boylan and Saxon, 1998). It should come as no surprise that institutions engaging in sound developmental education practice had much better outcomes than those that did not.

This situation illustrates one of the problems in looking at national or statewide outcomes studies as a measure of developmental education impact. In any given state or region, some campuses do a good job of designing and implementing developmental education, and others do a poor job. When data from all these are aggregated, the results are typically mediocre. Essentially the research indicates that developmental programs employing sound organizational and teaching strategies have been consistently linked to higher passing and completion rates in courses, better student grades, and higher rates of retention.

## Policy Issues in Developmental Education

We believe that developmental education is widely debated primarily because the public and many lawmakers confuse it with remediation. Few people would argue against the assessment of entering college students' academic skills. Few would deny that college students ought to have access to tutoring. And few would advocate elimination of services such as learning laboratories, study skills and strategies courses, critical thinking, or other short-term workshops. These are all common and, for the most part, widely accepted features of contemporary postsecondary education. These are also common features of contemporary developmental education.

Yet criticism of remedial courses is widespread. Parents and students complain that participation in remediation delays college completion. Legislators complain that remedial courses should not be offered on university campuses and argue that the public should not be asked to pay twice to have the same content taught. Many lawmakers and higher education executive officers argue that remedial courses should be relegated to the community college.

Unfortunately, discussions of remediation among lawmakers and higher education executive officers are more often driven by political considerations than by facts or sound educational policy (Breneman and Haarlow, 1998). It is a fact, for instance, that almost one-third of the nation's college students enter their institutions without prerequisite knowledge and skill in one or more content areas (National Center for Education Statistics, 1996). This lack of preparation among entering students is well documented through a variety of assessment tests. No amount of discussion or debate will make this fact disappear.

**Is the Need for Developmental Education of Recent Origin?**  The need for developmental education is not a new trend. The need for it does not result simply from the 1965 Higher Education Act, which opened the doors of higher education to nontraditional students (Cross, 1976). Although this act increased the numbers of nontraditional and underprepared students entering colleges and universities, it increased even more the numbers of traditional and fully prepared students who participated in higher education. Casazza and Silverman (1996), Maxwell (1997), and many others have clearly documented that the need for developmental education in U.S. colleges and universities has existed since the mid-1800s. In fact, modern developmental education traces its origins to the University of Wisconsin's college preparatory program in 1849 (Brier, 1984).

This need has changed little in the past two decades. In 1983, the National Center for Education Statistics reported that nearly a third of entering college students placed in one or more remedial courses in 1982 (National Center for Education Statistics, 1983). Using 1995 data, the center reported that this percentage had not changed significantly in the intervening thirteen years (National Center for Education Statistics, 1996). About one out of three entering students still places in one or more developmental courses.

Underprepared students have been with us in higher education for at least 150 years, and so have programs designed to meet their needs. Anyone who believes that they represent a new trend has a poor grasp of the history of U.S. higher education.

**Can the Need for Developmental Education Be Eliminated?** Only two things might reduce the need for developmental education in colleges and universities: a dramatic improvement in the quality of college preparation provided by public schools or a dramatic downsizing of postsecondary education.

Although it is to be hoped that the nation's public schools may eventually improve the level of their graduates' skills, this is not likely to happen in the foreseeable future. The task of taking millions of children from an incredible variety of social, cultural, economic, and ethnic backgrounds into public schools at age five and turning them out fully prepared for college twelve years later is a daunting one. It is not surprising that the majority of our public schools have been daunted by it.

The thirteen years between the two National Center for Education Statistics studies in college-level remediation mark what is probably the most aggressive period of school reform efforts in the nation's history. Although these efforts continue, they have yet to reduce the percentage of underprepared students entering postsecondary education.

The second option for reducing remediation is to refuse to admit students who need it. Because the majority of those needing remediation are from lower socioeconomic backgrounds (Boylan and Saxon, 1998), such a refusal might seriously limit educational opportunity for the poor. Because ethnic minorities are overrepresented among the nation's poor (Dalaker, 1999), such a refusal might seriously limit educational opportunity for minorities. And because there is a strong relationship between the educational attainment of its citizens and the economic prosperity of a state or region (Lavin and Hyllegard, 1996; McCabe and Day, 1998), such a refusal might stifle the economic development of some states and regions. These arguments do not even address the logistical problems and the political and economic consequences of downsizing the nation's colleges and universities by a factor of almost one-third. In short, downsizing is not a particularly attractive option.

**Hasn't the Public Already Paid Once for Developmental Education?** This argument is seriously flawed. The percentage of high school graduates who have completed a college preparatory curriculum has increased markedly in the past decade to a record high of 43 percent (Stratton, 1998). The public has not paid for college preparation twice. It has not even paid for it once. The public has paid for 43 percent of American high school graduates to take college preparatory courses.

Among those who graduate from high school, 62 percent will go on to college (Stratton, 1998). This suggests there is a difference of 19 percent between the percentage of high school graduates who took the courses that would have prepared them for college and those who actually attend college. These figures represent only recent high school graduates and do not count adult learners who may have attended high school ten or twenty or more years ago when taking college preparatory courses was far less prevalent than it is today. Adult learners, however, represent the fastest growing group of students in American higher education.

The issue, therefore, is not whether there is a need for developmental education in American higher education. It is likely that developmental education will continue to be necessary for the foreseeable future. From the standpoint of educational policy the issues should be who should provide developmental education and how it should be provided.

**Who Should Provide Developmental Education?** If by developmental education, we are referring to tutoring, study strategies, freshman seminars, and learning assistance centers, then the answer is *all higher education institutions*. The more selective an institution is, the less need it will have for some of these services. Nevertheless, even Harvard and the University of California at Berkeley provide tutoring and a variety of other services to assist students in making the adjustment to college and improving their academic performance.

If, by developmental education, we are referring to noncredit remedial courses teaching content clearly below college level, then the answer is *some higher education institutions*. The most selective institutions should not need to offer such courses, nor should the public and private research and flagship state universities. Essentially, the more selective an institution is, the less need it has for remedial courses.

This leaves two categories of institutions: less selective public and private four-year institutions, and community colleges. Four-year institutions of moderate to low selectivity serve a critical function in higher education. They make the opportunity for a baccalaureate degree and its social and economic benefits available to students who do not qualify for more prestigious institutions. In such institutions, it is likely that at least a third of entering students will not have all the skills necessary to be successful in college without some form of academic assistance (National Center for Education Statistics, 1996). If such institutions are to fill their niche in our higher education system, they must admit some poorly prepared students and must provide some means of supporting these students. We believe that virtually any institution with average entering student SAT scores of 1000 or less should provide some form of remediation.

Community colleges serve as a pathway to a baccalaureate degree for many students whose family, financial, or social circumstances prevent them from attending a four-year institution. They also provide education and training for those who have no intention of seeking a baccalaureate degree but still seek the benefits of postsecondary education. Both of these groups are likely to require substantial amounts of developmental education, including remediation. Community colleges are currently the primary provider of developmental education (Knopp, 1996), and the need for them to do so will continue. It is unreasonable to expect that any major changes in the preparation of high school graduates or the educational needs of adult learners will be substantial enough in the coming decades to allow community colleges to get out of the business of developmental education. The answer to this question therefore is that less selective universities as well as community colleges will need to provide developmental education courses and services well into the next millennium.

**How Should Developmental Education Be Provided?** Although the need for developmental education courses and services is likely to continue, it is entirely possible that the numbers of students who need to participate in them may be reduced. In order to do so, several actions may be required on the part of the nation's colleges and universities as well as its public schools. A few of the more promising means of accomplishing this goal are described below.

*Engage in expanded articulation and collaboration among high schools, colleges, and universities.* Few high school students are thoroughly familiar with the demands of college. Few recognize the difference between high school and college expectations. Too many students believe that earning a C in high school algebra will prepare them to take college-level mathematics courses.

The best way to resolve these problems is for high school and college instructors to collaborate in setting standards and expectations for college-bound students. Currently there is little connection between high school and college curriculums. State school officials and state and local politicians establish the high school curriculum. Passing standards for high school exit examinations are often set at the tenth-grade level.

The faculty of postsecondary institutions establish the college curriculum. The entry standards for college courses are often set at the twelfth-grade level. This means that there is often a disconnection between high school exit standards and college entry standards. Greater communication between those who teach courses at the high school and college levels needs to take place in order to develop a seamless curriculum without content and skill boundaries between high school and college expectations.

*Use more noncognitive assessment to determine who may participate in non-course-based developmental education.* Colleges and universities generally do an effective job of assessing entering students' cognitive skills through a variety of placement tests. In many cases, they do not do as good a job of assessing students' noncognitive or affective characteristics, such as motivation, attitude toward learning, or learning styles. These, however, are the very characteristics that determine whether a student will perform better in a sixteen-week developmental course or through enrollment in the regular college-level course supported by tutoring or other non-course-based interventions. As a result, an unknown number of entering students are placed in developmental courses when they might profit just as well from some other form of intervention.

If colleges and universities were to do a better job of assessing students' noncognitive characteristics, they might be able to identify those who need the structure of a sixteen-week course and those who might be successful with less intensive intervention. Simply providing more tutoring or workshops on study skills and strategies to these students might reduce their need to take developmental courses.

*Provide more alternatives to traditional remedial courses.* If colleges and universities are to reduce the number of students taking developmental courses, they will have to provide more alternatives to these courses. They frequently offer numerous sections of developmental courses because processing groups of students through a structured course is the most efficient way of handling large numbers of students. Alternatives to developmental courses are, however, available, and many of them have proved to be highly successful.

A reduction in developmental course participation for students requires an investment of more time and energy in alternatives such as student success courses, freshman seminars, learning assistance centers, supplemental instruction, or the integration of strategic learning techniques into the first-year curriculum. For students falling in the upper third of the developmental education course placement distribution, these techniques can provide a successful alternative to a sixteen-week course (Boylan, 1999). This is particularly true when advisers are well trained in the interpretation of noncognitive instruments and a variety of alternatives to developmental courses are made available.

*Improve developmental instruction so that greater numbers of students pass their courses on the first attempt.* Even if these innovations were to proliferate in American higher education, there would still be a need for some developmental courses. The National Center for Education Statistics (1996) reports that about 75 percent of students enrolled in developmental courses pass them within one year. This means that a fairly large number of students taking developmental courses do not pass them on their first attempt.

Admittedly, some students will be unable to pass developmental courses. However, several studies have reported that developmental courses are frequently taught by adjunct or part-time faculty with little training to prepare them to teach in developmental classrooms (Boylan, Bonham, Claxton, and Bliss, 1992; Boylan and Saxon, 1998; Roueche and Roueche, 1993;

Roueche and Roueche, 1999). Our contention is that many students who fail developmental courses might be successful if they had appropriate instruction. They key to reducing failure rates in developmental courses is to improve the quality of instruction by investing more heavily in the training of the part-time and adjunct faculty who teach these courses. As Pat Cross has pointed out, there is a strong relationship between the quality of teaching and the quality of learning (Angelo and Cross, 1991). Improving the quality of teaching available to developmental students cannot help but improve the quality of their learning.

## Conclusion

It is altogether likely that the spectrum of activities known as developmental education will continue to be part of U.S. higher education. In spite of the debate surrounding remediation, eliminating developmental education is not a viable alternative. The social, political, educational, and economic consequences of such a move range from merely uncomfortable to bordering on disastrous.

Several themes emerge and reemerge throughout this chapter. One is that developmental students represent fairly typical adults whose academic problems have been encountered and resolved for at least 150 years. Another theme is that the use of sound, research-based, developmental education practices can yield positive outcomes for students. A third is that much of the public and political debate over remedial and developmental education is fraught with misconceptions about what it is, whom it serves, and how it works.

We see the debate over developmental education as positive. We hope it will promote understanding of the field and the students it serves. It may also clarify misconceptions and eventually lead to reasonable and practical solutions to the problem of underpreparedness among a large number of students in postsecondary education.

A debate conducted with clarity, understanding, and knowledge of the causes and cures of a given phenomenon can only have a positive outcome. Unfortunately, the debate over developmental education was not typically characterized by these factors during the 1990s. We hope that the information presented in this chapter may help policymakers and administrators enter into the debate with a better understanding of the complex factors that have required American colleges and universities to offer developmental education programs and will no doubt require similar offerings in the future.

## References

Adelman, C. "The Truth About Remedial Work: It's More Complex Than Windy Rhetoric and Simple Solutions Suggest." *Chronicle of Higher Education*, Oct. 4, 1996, p. A56.

Angelo, T., and Cross, K. P. *Classroom Assessment Techniques*. San Francisco: Jossey-Bass, 1991.

Bloom, B. S. *Human Characteristics and School Learning*. New York: McGraw-Hill, 1976.

Boylan, H. R. "Exploring Alternatives to Remediation." *Journal of Developmental Education,* 1999, *22* (3), 2–11.

Boylan, H., Bliss, L., and Bonham, B. "Program Components and Their Relationship to Student Performance." *Journal of Developmental Education,* 1997, *20* (3), 2–9.

Boylan, H., and Bonham, B. "Improving Developmental Instruction: Lessons from 30 Years of Research." Paper presented at the National Association for Developmental Education Conference, Detroit, Feb. 1999.

Boylan, H., Bonham, B., and Bliss, L. "Who Are the Developmental Students?" *Research in Developmental Education,* 1994, *11* (2), 1–4.

Boylan, H., Bonham, B., Claxton, C., and Bliss, L. "The State of the Art in Developmental Education: Report of a National Study." Paper presented at the First National Conference on Research in Developmental Education, Charlotte, N.C., Nov. 1992.

Boylan, H. R., and Saxon, D. P. *An Evaluation of Developmental Education in Texas Colleges and Universities*. Austin, Tex.: Texas Higher Education Coordinating Board, 1998.

Brier, E. "Bridging the Academic Preparation Gap." *Journal of Developmental Education,* 1984, *8* (1), 2–5.

Breneman, D. W., and Haarlow, W. N. *Remediation in Higher Education: A Symposium.* Fordham Report: 1998. Available online at http://www.edexcellence.net/library/remed.html

Casazza, M., and Silverman, S. *Learning Assistance and Developmental Education*. San Francisco: Jossey-Bass, 1996.

Claxton, C. S. "Learning Styles and Instructional Development." Paper presented at the Kellogg Institute for the Training and Certification of Developmental Educators, Appalachian State University, Boone, N.C., July 1994.

Cross, K. P. *Accent on Learning*. San Francisco: Jossey-Bass, 1976.

Dalaker, J. *Poverty in the United States 1998*. Washington, D.C.: U.S. Census Bureau, 1999. Available online at http://www.census.gov/prod/99pubs/P60-207.pdf.

Donovan, R. *Alternatives to the Revolving Door: Report of National Project II*. Bronx, N.Y.: Bronx Community College, 1974.

Hardin, C. "Who Belongs in College: A Second Look." In J. Higbee and P. Dwinnel (eds.), *Developmental Education: Preparing Successful College Students*. Columbia, S.C.: National Resource Center for the First-Year Experience and Students in Transition, 1998.

Kiemig, R. T. *Raising Academic Standards: A Guide to Learning Improvement*. Washington, D.C.: Association for the Study of Higher Education, 1983.

Knopp, L. "Remedial Education: An Undergraduate Student Profile." *American Council on Education Research Briefs,* 1996, *6* (8), 1–11.

Kulik, C-L., Kulik, J., and Schwalb, B. (1983). "College Programs for High Risk and Disadvantaged Students: A Meta-Analysis of Findings." *Review of Educational Research,* 1983, *53*(3), 397–414.

Lavin, D., and Hyllegard, L. *Changing the Odds: Open Admissions and The Life Changes of The Disadvantaged*. New Haven, Conn.: Yale University Press, 1996.

Maxwell, M. *Improving Student Learning Skills*. Clearwater, Fla.: H and H Publishing Co., 1997.

McCabe, R., and Day, P. *Developmental Education: A Twenty-First Century Social and Economic Imperative*. Mission Viejo, Calif.: League for Innovation in the Community College, 1998.

McMullin, W. E., and Young, J. "A Solution: Will an Attendance Policy Keep More Students in Class?" *Assessment Update,* 1994, *6* (6), 6–7.

Minnesota State Colleges and Universities. *Developmental Education Outcomes at Minnesota Community Colleges, May 1996*. St. Paul: Minnesota State Colleges and Universities, 1996.

Morante, E. (1989). "Selecting Tests and Placing Students." *Journal of Developmental Education*, 1989, *13* (2), 2–6.

National Center for Education Statistics. *The Condition of Education, 1983*. Washington, D.C.: U. S. Department of Education, Office of Educational Research and Improvement, 1983.

National Center for Education Statistics. *Remedial Courses in Higher Education in the Fall of 1995*. Washington, D.C.: U. S. Office of Education, Office of Educational Research and Improvement, 1996.

Nelson, R. "Establishing Personal Management Training in Developmental Education and First Year Curricula." In J. Higbee and P. Dwinnel (eds.), *Developmental Education: Preparing Successful College Students*. Columbia, S.C.: National Resource Center for the First-Year Experience and Students in Transition, 1998.

Roueche, J. E., and Snow, J. J. *Overcoming Learning Problems*. San Francisco: Jossey-Bass, 1977.

Roueche, J. E., and Roueche, S. *Between a Rock and a Hard Place: The At-Risk Student in the Open Door College*. Washington, D.C.: Community College Press, 1993.

Roueche, J., and Roueche, S. *High Stakes, High Performance: Making Remediation Work*. Washington, D.C.: American Association of Community Colleges, 1999.

Sedlacek, W. E. "Black Students on White Campuses: 20 Years of Research." *Journal of College Student Personnel*, 1987, *19* (3), 242–248.

Stahl, N., Simpson, M., and Hayes, C. "Ten Recommendations from Research for Teaching High-Risk College Students." *Journal of Developmental Education*, 1992, *16* (1), 2-10.

Starks, G. "Retention and Developmental Education: What the Research Has to Say." In M. Maxwell (ed.), *From Access to Success*. Clearwater, Fla.: H and H Publishing Company, 1994.

Stratton, C. B. (1998). "Transitions in Developmental Education." In J. Higbee and P. Dwinnel (eds.), *Developmental Education: Preparing Successful College Students*. Columbia, S.C.: National Resource Center for the First-Year Experience and Students in Transition, 1998.

Upcraft, M. L., and Gardner, J. N. *The Freshman Year Experience*. San Francisco: Jossey-Bass, 1989.

Weinstein, C., and others. "The Impact of a Course in Strategic Learning on the Long-Term Retention of College Students." In J. Higbee and P. Dwinnel (eds.), *Developmental Education: Preparing Successful College Students*. Columbia, S.C.: National Resource Center for the First-Year Experience and Students in Transition, 1998.

HUNTER R. BOYLAN *is director of the National Center for Developmental Education and professor of higher education at Appalachian State University, Boone, N.C.*

BARBARA S. BONHAM *is coordinator of Higher Education Graduate Programs and professor of higher education at Appalachian State University, Boone, N.C.*

STEPHEN R. WHITE *is associate professor of educational foundations in the Department of Leadership and Educational Studies at Appalachian State University, Boone, N.C.*

*7* *The Texas Academic Skills Program, like many other*
*such programs nationally, has become the lightning rod*
*for a quality of learning situation it did not create. To*
*assuage public concerns about remediation, sustained*
*reform of the whole education system is needed rather*
*than shortsighted and misplaced concerns about reform*
*of the testing instruments.*

# Remediation in Texas: A Prototype for National Reform?

*Susan R. Griffith, Joseph M. Meyer*

The Texas Academic Skills Program (TASP) was established in 1987 in the Texas Education Code as a diagnostic tool to ensure that all students in Texas are provided with the basic skills to compete in college. Program funding from the state has grown more than fourfold from the $38.6 million appropriated for 1988–1989, to $172 million in 1998–1999 (Breneman and Haarlow, 1998); adjusted for inflation, the increase is 179 percent. At the same time, enrollment of college freshmen increased only 6 percent (Texas Higher Education Coordinating Board [THECB], PREP System, 1999), but the enrollment in remedial courses increased 81 percent (Omar Lopez, personal communication, May 5, 1999). (See Figure 7.1.)

After a dozen years of experience, it is appropriate to take stock of the TASP: to review its history and results and look to its future. Many other states are also taking a critical look at their remedial programs, looking to cutting-edge states such as Texas for solutions to this most difficult, expensive, and escalating problem.

## A State at Risk

In the early 1980s, Texas, like many other states, instituted an admissions test for students entering educator preparation programs. The Pre-Professional Skills Test (PPST) results from 1984 to 1986 were alarming: 30 percent failed the test on the first try, and in subsequent testings, half continued to fail (THECB, 1986). The SAT and ACT scores of the education students and the general student body at a large (20,000 students), comprehensive institution in the state were "virtually the same," according to the chair of

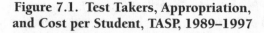

**Figure 7.1. Test Takers, Appropriation, and Cost per Student, TASP, 1989–1997**

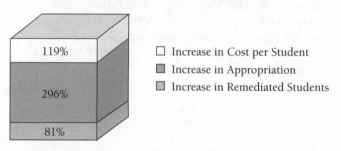

the THECB's Special Committee on Basic Skills. The PPST failure rate was extrapolated to the entire Texas student population (Alpert, Gorth, and Allan, 1989). Fearing that 30 percent or more of all Texas college students might be at risk, the THECB established its first committee on testing led by the chair of the Coordinating Board. According to the assistant commissioner of THECB, the committee on testing was charged "to examine the feasibility and desirability of implementing a test for public higher education students in the state…to provide a measurement of both the quality of teaching and the quality of learning in the system" (Alpert, Gorth, and Allan, 1989, p. 13).

In 1986, the report of the testing committee of the THECB, *A Generation of Failure: The Case for Testing and Remediation in Texas Higher Education* (1986), showed that the disturbing failure rate of PPST was not confined to education majors. Just as predicted by the chair of the Special Committee on Basic Skills, 30 percent of all Texas high school students were unprepared for college. Considering that Texas is a below-average producer of undergraduate degrees in the United States, this situation did not bode well for the future.

In 1987, the Seventieth Texas Legislature created TASP. That test, according to a former member of the Texas House of Representatives and chair of its Higher Education Committee, was to answer the question, "Are we getting our money's worth?" from the investment in higher education. That Texas representative then warned that the institutions would be held responsible for student success, since the students met the institutional admission criteria. If those students cannot pass the basic skills test, the institutions "must offer some kind of remediation to address those deficiencies if, in fact, they do exist" (Alpert, Gorth, and Allan, 1989).

In the spring of 1987, section 51.306 of the Texas Education Code outlined the requirements for testing all freshmen entering Texas public colleges and universities and offering remedial courses for students failing to meet the statewide standard. The goal of TASP was to ensure that all students would possess the basic preparatory skills in writing, reading, and math to perform at the undergraduate level (THECB, 1995). "The key assumption behind the Texas Legislature is that students may lack the skills, not the ability, to do college-level work," said the coordinating board's director of the TASP (Alpert, Gorth, and Allan, 1989, p. 29).

## Developing the Test

In September 1987, the THECB contracted with National Evaluation Systems (NES) in Amherst, Massachusetts, to develop and administer the test. Over four thousand Texas educators were involved in the process through survey efforts and the many committees and fora convened across the state. Nearly seven hundred faculty were directly involved in TASP committees, and their representation was equally split between two-year and four-year institutions; one-third was minority (Alpert, Gorth, and Allan, 1989). THECB and the Texas Education Agency established a content advisory committee for each of the three content areas: reading, writing, and math. A bias review panel was established to ensure fairness for gender and ethnic subgroups of students. Over three hundred educators participated in meetings held in nine regions of Texas to ensure broad participation. The Coordinating Board also formed many committees and review panels to focus on the impacts and aspects of the TASP program, including faculty development, academic advising, and developmental education (NES, 1998).

Input from these committees and a series of surveys conducted by NES, sent to over four thousand faculty, resulted in the list of skills to be tested by the TASP (Alpert, Gorth, and Allan, 1989). The test questions to assess these skills were piloted at colleges and universities. Revisions were made to the test questions based on feedback from the faculty who reviewed the statistical performance of the test questions. To improve the TASP test, new questions are regularly developed, reviewed by the Content Advisory Committee and the Bias Review Panel, and pilot-tested on Texas students.

## Which Students Are Tested

When the TASP went into effect in the fall of 1989, it affected all students who entered public colleges or universities with no prior collegiate hours and who enrolled for at least nine semester credit hours or the equivalent. It also affected students with fewer than sixty semester credit hours who transferred into an institution without yet taking the test. The majority of Texas's freshmen took the TASP and were required to do so before they accumulated fifteen semester credit hours; in 1993, the limit was lowered to nine hours. Students are required to pass all three sections of the TASP before they can enroll in upper-level classes (for their sixty-first semester credit hour at a senior college), or before they can graduate from a two-year institution. Students pay for these tests themselves, unless financial need is determined, in which case the state pays the cost. Students must retake any failed section until they pass all sections. They are placed in remedial instruction (course-based or non-course-based) upon failure.

In fall 1993, for the first time, students who performed at certain high levels on the Scholastic Aptitude Test (SAT), the American College Test (ACT), or the Texas Assessment of Academic Skills (TAAS) were exempt from the test. The scores that would allow an exemption were changed in 1995 and again in 1997. (See Table 7.1.) Both times the scores for exemption were lowered, allowing more students to avoid taking the TASP.

## Nature of the TASP Test

Students are provided with up to five hours during each testing session and may work on any or all sections of the test during that time frame. The reading comprehension section has about a dozen selections of 300 to 750 words each. Students answer approximately fifty questions related to these selections. The math section also contains about fifty questions covering fundamental math, algebra, geometry, and problem solving. The writing section consists of two parts: a 300- to 600-word essay and multiple-choice questions regarding elements of effective writing (THECB, 1995). A test study guide is available, and accommodations are made for students with disabilities. You can obtain an order form for the test guide and answers to frequently asked questions at www.tasp.nesinc.com. (NES, 1998).

## Outcome

The 1986 *Generation of Failure* study indicated that about one-third of Texas students were unprepared for college. In practice, however, the TASP test has steadily identified over 50 percent of nonexempt students who must enroll in at least one developmental course or other remediation service (THECB, 1995; Boylan and Saxon, 1998). These figures suggest that up to nearly half the students in Texas public schools are being graduated from high school unable to conduct college-level work without remedial help.

In response, Texas has appropriated increasingly larger amounts of money to fund the college-level remediation courses and service needs diagnosed by the TASP test. For the 1988–1989 biennium, Texas appropriated $36.8 million for remediation; by 1998–1999, the total had risen to $172 million, an increase of nearly 350 percent. Adjusted for inflation, the increase was 179 percent. At the same time, the enrollment of freshmen in public higher education had increased by only 6 percent. These costs are being incurred for students who have already graduated from high school, for which the public also has paid before.

In addition, the cost to students has risen. In 1989, the fee for each TASP test session was $24; in 1996, $26; in 1998 it was $29. Students do

**Table 7.1. Minimum Test Scores for Exemption from the TASP Test**

| Test | July 1993 | April 1995 | Fall 1997 |
|---|---|---|---|
| ACT composite | 29+ | 29+ | 23+ |
| Math | 27+ | 22+ | 19+ |
| English | 27+ | 22+ | 19+ |
| | | | |
| SAT composite | 1270+ | 1270+ | 1070+ |
| Verbal | 620+ | 620+ | 500+ |
| Math | 560+ | 560+ | 500+ |
| | | | |
| TAAS/TLI | | | |
| Writing | 1800+ | 1800+ | 1770+ |
| Reading | 91+ | 90+ | 86+ |
| Math | 87+ | 87+ | 89+ |

*Notes:* The 1993 SAT scores were recentered to compare with later scores.

The 1993 Texas Assessment of Academic Skills scores were converted to the Texas Learning Index scale, which was used in 1995 and 1997.

*Sources:* http://www.thecb.tx.us/divisions/GRPI/cbreps/JulSep1993.htm#b; THECB Rules: Chapter 5, Subchapter P, sec. 5.313(b)(2)(A-D).

not pay for the test a single time; if they fail, they must pay each time they retake the test. Other costs include additional tuition and fees for course-based remediation, time spent in non-course-based remediation, increases in the time to graduation, and the psychic impact of repeated failure.

## Comparisons over Time

It is hard to make comparisons of TASP performance and remediation results over time, since the rules of the game have changed so often.

In 1993, the Texas legislature amended the Texas Education Code to exempt students from taking the TASP if they had certain ACT, SAT, or TAAS scores. (See Table 7.1.) Exempting these high-scoring students from taking the TASP leaves less well-prepared students in the pool when comparisons are made from year to year. Then the test was made longer and "slightly more difficult" (THECB, 1996). Instead of allowing students to take up to fifteen credit hours before taking the TASP, the time limit was now moved back to nine hours, so students were taking the test with less college experience under their belts (THECB, 1996). According to the Coordinating Board's 1995 report on the TASP (THECB, 1995), "These programmatic alterations have caused a dramatic change in the tested population, and less-prepared students are now attempting the examination, resulting in dramatically lower pass rates when compared with previous years."

In 1995, the standards for passing the TASP test were again increased. Before 1995, the passing score for writing, reading or math was 220; after

1995, reading and math passing scores increased to 230 (THECB, 1999). The exemption scores stayed virtually the same.

In 1997, the ACT, SAT, and TAAS test scores that allowed exemption from taking the TASP were reduced from earlier levels. Again, the result was that less well-prepared and less well-performing students were required to take the TASP. (See Figure 7.2.) The 1997 legislative session changed the rules to allow students who earned a B or better in a course related to the area of the TASP they failed to be exempted from retaking and passing the TASP test. Consequently, the pass rate for retaking the TASP test has declined artificially and rendered longitudinal analysis problematic at best.

Partially as a result of these numerous changes, the TASP test pass and remediation success rates have fallen over time. This does not mean necessarily that Texas college students are performing worse or that remediation is not working. It would be interesting to compare the stratum of students taking the test today with the same stratum in 1989, but that is not possible.

## Is TASP Working?

According to two independent reviews of the TASP program published in 1996 and 1998 by the National Center for Developmental Education (Boylan and others, 1996; Boylan and Saxon, 1998), the TASP program is valid: "Essentially, the TASP is basically a sound system supported by a sound assessment instrument. Unfortunately, implementation of this system by institutions is very uneven" (Boylan and Saxon, 1998). In short, the test has not failed; the institutions have badly used the test, often suggesting it is predictive rather than diagnostic, and the public schools are graduating and certifying a "product" that cannot meet minimal standards of academic competence. Unfortunately, the TASP test has become the lightning rod for results it did not create but largely inherited.

In their 1996 assessment, the researchers concluded that remediation in Texas was working. They based this pronouncement on the fact that a good proportion of students who failed all or part of the TASP on their first try passed on their second try following remediation. As Table 7.2 shows, 42 percent to 75 percent of students passed the TASP on their second try following remediation. There are large differences, however, depending on the type of institution attended. The pass rate for the third attempt is lower: 31 percent for the math portion, 44 percent for the reading portion, and 64 percent for the writing portion.

Another way of gauging the success of remediation is the grade that students make in their first college English class following remediation in reading or writing. Most—60 to 74 percent—received a C or better in the class. However, only about one-third passed their first collegiate math course.

The 1998 assessment of TASP continues to report relatively poor statistics on Texas's college students. Again, the data and performance of students in remediation vary by type of institution, with students in the main

**Figure 7.2.  Relationship of the TASP Pass Rate and Exemption Rate**

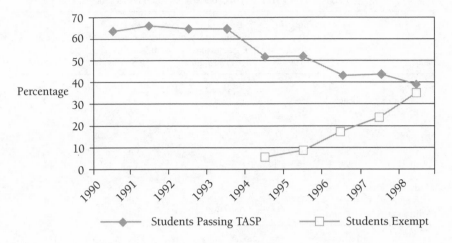

**Table 7.2.  Pass Rate on the Second Try
of the TASP Test Following Remediation**

| Test Section | All Institutions (Percentage) | Two-Year Colleges and Universities (Percentage) | Four-Year Colleges and Universities (Percentage) |
|---|---|---|---|
| Math | 42 | 39 | 62 |
| Reading | 58 | 55 | 80 |
| Writing | 75 | 72 | 97 |

performing better in senior than community colleges following placement in developmental courses (Table 7.3).

For the 1998 assessment, the consultants for the first time looked at the performance of students whose TASP test scores indicated they were severely deficient in academic skills. A student with a score below 180 on any subpart of the TASP was studied separately. Even with a higher proportion of these students, labeled by the researchers as "unlikely…to pass the TASP Test without at least two or three semesters of developmental education," senior colleges had greater success rates following remediation than did community colleges.

## Public Policy

Analyzing TASP data is difficult, and making comparisons over time is nearly impossible, since the test passing score, exemption and retake criteria, and

**Table 7.3.  Performance of Community College
and University Students on the TASP Test**

| Subject | Percentage in Developmental Courses, Fall 1996 | Percentage Passing TASP, First Attempt After Remediation | Percentage Passing Developmental Course and Later TASP Section | Percentage with TASP Score Below 180 |
|---|---|---|---|---|
| Reading | | | | |
| Community College | 38 | 8 | 33 | 10 |
| University | 27 | 11 | 76 | 14 |
| Writing | | | | |
| Community College | 40 | 10 | 66 | 10 |
| University | 48 | 21 | 86 | 15 |
| Math | | | | |
| Community College | 62 | 12 | 30 | 14 |
| University | 64 | 20 | 65 | 16 |

timing of the test have changed over time. However, these realities do not hinder public policy experts and politicians who use the data at face value to evaluate the program and make recommendations. Whether their analyses are statistically valid is irrelevant, since they have a political voice that ostensibly reflects their constituency. Again the TASP test has all too often become the lightning rod for a set of conditions and costs created and penetrated by other agencies of society.

In 1996, a Texas State representative filed a bill to hold school districts liable for remediation costs incurred by colleges and universities (Robbins, 1996). A similar bill was filed in the House during the 1999 regular legislative session. Indeed, a review of information found on the Web site Texas Legislature Online revealed many political challenges to the current system. Other bills filed during this session ranged from those seeking total abolition of the TASP, to allowing other diagnostic tests, to increasing the exemptions, to increasing the time allowed for the test, and to making the tests free for all needy students. In short, unhappiness about the TASP is a common theme, covering all political philosophies, ethnicities, and income levels.

In 1997 the Texas Public Policy Foundation commissioned a paper (Parker and Ratliff, 1997) on the TASP program. The authors cite many variables in making their case that the public school systems in Texas need to be held more accountable for the dismal performance of their students when they attend college. Among their findings were these:

The failure rate for first-time, full-time students increased by 16 percent from fiscal year 1992 to fiscal year 1995.
In 1994, nearly half (48.4 percent) of students failed one or more sections of the test.

Community colleges are shouldering an increasing burden of remediation.
   They increased from providing 5.3 million hours of remedial course work
   in fiscal year 1987 to 21.3 million in fiscal year 1995, an increase of 400
   percent. The numbers at senior institutions declined during this period.
For the 1990 cohort, over 86 percent of remediated students did not graduate in six years from a senior college or in three years from a community
   college.

The authors used these data to advocate for increased accountability of public school systems and for school vouchers.

## The Fairness Issue

The THECB consultants in 1996 (Boylan and others, 1996) found that the
TASP test is "fair" to all ethnic groups and genders despite a popular per-
ception that it disproportionately negatively affects minorities, another common charge levied against the test. Despite these findings, there are gaps in
the pass rate surrounding remediation when examined by ethnic group. As
Table 7.4 indicates, the rate for passing the TASP after remediation is higher
for Anglo students than for non-Anglo students.

   The consultants admit that although the TASP may be fair for all ethnicities, it is more effective for whites. They suggest the following reasons
for poor performance by non-Anglos, which are beyond the scope of the
TASP: poor preparation in high school, uneven quality of remediation in
colleges and universities, and the fact that college-level remediation is not
tailored to different learning styles required for successful remediation (see
Chapter Six). These factors would also contribute to the lower performance
of community colleges, since overall they enroll greater proportions of non-
Anglo students than senior colleges and universities do.

## Conclusions and Recommendations

Attacking the TASP because it identifies students who are unprepared for
college and may or may not succeed after remediation is akin to killing the
messenger. The test, rather than the underlying conditions that it identifies
but did not create, has become the object of hostility. "Although remediation efforts may be costly, the need for these efforts would be present
whether the TASP exists or not. The TASP is simply a mirror" (Boylan and
others, 1996). The test is reliable and valid, and it identifies students lacking sufficient preparation (diagnosis, not prediction) for college, which it
was designed to do. Further, it indicts the public school systems in the state,
which are responsible in part for the mounting hostility of the public and
policymakers. Rather than throw out the test, Texas should use the TASP to
improve secondary school performance. After all, the primary purpose of
the test is to be diagnostic, for either individuals or institutions.

**Table 7.4.  Performance on the TASP Test
After Remediation, by Ethnic Group**

| Ethnicity | Math Score (%) | Reading Score (%) | Writing Score (%) |
|-----------|----------------|-------------------|-------------------|
| Anglo | 46 | 62 | 80 |
| Black | 35 | 48 | 78 |
| Hispanic | 34 | 57 | 73 |

When one looks solely at the cost, there are reasons to search for a better solution. As shown in Figure 7.1, between 1989 and 1997, the number of test takers increased 81 percent, the appropriation for remediation increased 296 percent, and the cost per student increased 119 percent. While one may argue that the money is well spent, because students would have otherwise performed very poorly or flunked out of college, the question remains: Is this the best, most efficient, or most effective time in a student's school career to spend that money? Furthermore, is this paying twice for the results that should have been produced in high school? Poor remedial education costs more than "good" remedial education.

Initially the Texas legislature threatened to hold colleges and universities, rather than the school systems, accountable for student failure on basic skills tests (Alpert, Gorth, and Allan, 1989). The institutions responded and set up remediation programs. Now the public in Texas and elsewhere are outraged—and rightly so—by the onerous increasing cost of remediation, which many characterize as "paying for high school twice." Currently the national focus has shifted more to the supplier, with demands that the public schools improve secondary education, such that remediation at the college level will slowly disappear. In other words, the origin of the problem lies not so much in postsecondary education but in the precollege preparation of these students.

Some recommendations for improving college-level remediation, in the short run, and the public schools, in the long run, are offered here and have validity in settings far beyond Texas:

Considering that students are more likely to pass the TASP after successful completion of developmental courses in senior colleges, the state, through the Coordinating Board, should identify and disseminate best practices in remediation and implement and fund such replication programs in junior colleges and in senior colleges that are less successful overall.

Since the poorer performance of non-Anglo students seems to be linked to poorer preparation in the high schools, Texas and other states must accelerate their efforts to provide equal educational opportunity and demand equal results when equal resources are provided.

The state should consider publicizing TASP scores by school district to encourage improvement in secondary schools.

Because some students who graduate from high school with a B average cannot pass the TASP, the state should consider holding the school districts accountable for the cost of remediation borne by the state, the colleges, and universities. In short, the state should require and demand "product liability" from schools that graduate students. The high school diploma must indicate a certain minimum level of proficiency, not social promotion. Accountability may have to be painful to be productive, at least initially. This approach will become even more important, and ultimately more embarrassing and expensive, to the states.
The business community should work in greater partnership with the high schools and colleges and universities to solve this problem. Conversely, the business community should place increased pressure on schools and legislature to seek a solution rather than expecting the college level to remedy the situation.

If Texas and other states do not improve their public schools, which are largely the source of this problem, then the TASP and similar diagnostic tests in other states will continue to identify an unacceptable proportion of college students—who have been admitted under the college and university entrance criteria—as unprepared or underprepared to succeed in college. Nothing will dissipate the heat from an ineffective system better than positive results and sustained reform rather than visceral or politically motivated intrusions that do little to assuage public concerns about the nature and practice of remediation. In the long run the economic future of the United States and the continuation of our democratic concepts depend on such constructive proposals.

## References

Alpert, R. T., Gorth, W. P., and Allan, R. G. (eds.). *Assessing Basic Academic Skills in Higher Education: The Texas Approach.* Hillsdale, N.J.: Erlbaum, 1989.

Boylan, H. R., and others. *An Evaluation of the Texas Academic Skills Program (TASP).* Austin: Texas Higher Education Coordinating Board, 1996. Available at: http://www.thecb.state.tx.us/divisions/univ/tasp/boylans/boymain.htm.

Boylan, H. R., and Saxon, D. P. *An Evaluation of Developmental Education in Texas Public Colleges and Universities.* Available online at http://www.thecb.state.tx.us/divisions/univ/tasp/boylanz/, 1998.

Breneman, D. W., and Haarlow, W. N. Remedial Education: Costs and Consequences, with commentaries by Robert M. Costrell, David H. Ponitz, and Laurence Steinberg, 1998. Available at: http://edexcellence.net/library/remed.html.

National Evaluation Systems. Information About the Texas Academic Skills Program. 1998. Available at: http://www.tasp.nesinc.com/rg08info.htm.

Parker, A. E., and Ratliff, S. *Paying for Public High School Education Twice: Remediation in Texas Public Higher Education.* Austin: Texas Public Policy Foundation, May 1997. Available at: http://www.tppf.org/twice/texesu.htm.

Robbins, M. A. "College Remediation Costs May Be Passed to School Districts." *Amarillo Globe News,* Dec. 7, 1996.

Texas Education Code. 1987, Sec. 51.306.

Texas Higher Education Coordinating Board. *A Generation of Failure: The Case for Testing and Remediation in Texas Higher Education*. Austin: Texas Higher Education Coordinating Board, July 17, 1986.

Texas Higher Education Coordinating Board. *1989 PREP System Statistical Report*. Austin: Texas Higher Education Coordinating Board, 1989.

Texas Higher Education Coordinating Board. *TASP and the Effectiveness of Remediation. Annual Report*. Austin: Texas Higher Education Coordinating Board, 1995.

Texas Higher Education Coordinating Board. *TASP and the Effectiveness of Remediation*. Austin: Texas Higher Education Coordinating Board, 1996.

Texas Higher Education Coordinating Board. THECB Rules: Chapter 5, Subchapter P, 1999.

SUSAN R. GRIFFITH *is chief planning officer for the Council for South Texas Economic Progress, McAllen, Texas, a student loan servicing agency, and the South Texas Higher Education Authority, the oldest continuously operational secondary market for student loans in the United States.*

JOSEPH M. MEYER *is director of institutional research and planning at Southwest Texas State University in San Marcos, Texas.*

8

*Enrollment increases will add costs and new clienteles, and universities will find themselves struggling to maintain access unless they update or reform the remedial components of their curricula.*

# What the Future Holds

*Gerald H. Gaither*

There is a striking consensus among the seers who have been describing the college and university of the near future. The institution of 2010, they say, will be a mixture of unprecedented demographic and technological transformation as today's so-called minorities are becoming the new majority, and powerful digital capabilities are arriving daily with startling speed. These developments foreshadow great difficulties in managing the transition. It is no secret that a hot debate now rages across the United States about the role of remedial education, diversity, affirmative action, which students to recruit and educate, and the balance of public resources spent versus personal responsibility for education cost.

As the new century dawns, it brings with it twin versions of egalitarianism that deeply divide our attitudes toward recruitment, retention, and remediation. One version of egalitarianism, the *Jeffersonians,* believe in opportunity, gain, and growth on the basis of individual merit. They largely demand that the academy hold fast to its traditional roles, character, and mission. A second egalitarian theme in the American context is the *Jacksonian levelers,* who seek greater equality of result and condition. The Jacksonians are interested in closing the economic, social, and education gap between those at the top and those at the bottom, and they are willing to use the power of the state to accomplish these goals, using redistribution of income, whereas the Jeffersonians are suspicious of centralized power and state funding of social or remedial programs not based on clear individual merit. Society thus has a cluster of bipolar commitments tugging at both of these value dimensions as they affect recruitment, remediation, and retention (Balderston, 1995; Cohen, 1998). Some contemporary examples of this philosophical conflict are legal cases over preferential admissions (examples are *Adams* v. *Richardson,* 1973; *Bakke* v. *University of California,* 1978; and

New Directions for Higher Education, no. 108, Winter 1999 © Jossey-Bass Publishers

*Hopwood* v. *Texas,* 1996); legislative intrusion (for example, in California, Texas, and Georgia) in rewriting admission standards, traditionally a feature of campus governance; and federal involvement (through the Civil Rights Commission) against using standardized test scores in admission criteria. And in general, all Americans favor lots of education, but they are ambivalent about the use and cost of such egalitarian issues as retention, remediation, and greater access.

Sustaining a system of higher education that remains the envy of the rest of the world for its quality yet is open, effective, just, and inclusive will require a mixture of these two philosophies. Let the great public and private universities continue their graduate and research agenda, while the community and comprehensive colleges continue to respond to the demand for access. Certainly ours is an era marked by conflict—legal, political, and otherwise—of two competing philosophies of operating our systems of higher education. Those two philosophies illustrate the nature and depth of public resistance to the idea of any erosion of an intellectually demanding education, with students who are intellectually able, highly literate, and broadly knowledgeable. The great universities believe they will fail in their most precious responsibility to society: to foster in the best and brightest an insatiable taste for scholarship, ideas, and intellectual challenge and exchange, to foster creativity, as the primary principles that have historically underpinned the cultural and intellectual ideals of American higher education. The need for top-quality research and graduate study in a society that will become overwhelmingly knowledge based is a role that should not be sacrificed to the democratic mantra for access. Certainly these particular views do not reflect a consensus about the purposes of public higher education or the future roles of their recruiting, remediation, and retention programs.

The Jacksonians have revolutionized access to higher education since the end of World War II. At the end of World War II college enrollments were a mere 1 million college students; they have soared in a half-century to more than 14 million. The proportion of high school graduates entering college has risen from just over half in 1980 to 67 percent currently. In 1960, there were 2,026 colleges and universities—and today there are more than 3,600 institutions of higher education to accommodate the more than 14 million students, with a 30 percent increase in enrollment projected over the next two decades (see Chapter One). In California alone a tidal wave of new students—500,000 more than are enrolled today—will seek admission by 2010 (California Citizens, 1999).

These statistics tell a great American success story and force us to recognize the importance that postwar America placed on broad and equitable access to higher education. The concurrent pursuit of quantity and quality, in characteristic American fashion, was accepted as an inevitable challenge and a public responsibility. The challenges ahead include the certainty that current state resources will not be sufficient to pay for this new tidal wave, raising questions about who should pay, and growing differences over whether this new tidal wave should be accommodated. Overall support for higher education has unquestionably dropped, representing a $7.7 billion loss since 1990. State appropriations to higher education decreased sharply through the 1980s, with the tuition and fees making up the brunt of these cuts (Layzell and Caruthers, 1999). While modest appropriation increases generally occurred in the 1990s, recovery has not been adequate. Major public tuition increases in the near future seem probable and could exacerbate the problems of access and threaten to increase divisiveness along economic and racial lines.

This paean to access has a downside: a proliferation of institutions with graduates of uneven quality, of marginal students who sometimes took easy courses, under systems with subpar academic standards. Many of these students did get a degree, but did they get an education? In short, quality has not kept pace with educational opportunity. What is remarkable is just how little fundamental change this erosion in quality produced. Certainly a case can be made that it is not access or college graduates who are in short supply, but literate college graduates. The changing nature of academic activities to a technologically driven future suggests that the labor-intensive nature of current remediation practices could lead to more mediocrity, an intellectual wasteland, unless restructuring of the current approaches begins to occur. Otherwise future resistance could be intense and the political backlash threatening. Thus, greater access to higher education is under challenge, and future demographics suggest that opposition to remediation may increase. The forces opposing change are far more powerful than most realize.

To exacerbate the situation, these philosophical differences and discussions are taking place at the very time that a major demographic transformation is taking place. A 30 percent increase in the number of college-age students is expected over the next two decades, and California expects a half-million new students in the next decade. As Murdock and Hoque observed in Chapter One, most of that new population will be minorities who will be less academically prepared, less well off financially, and probably in need of greater government support than in the past. Costs will outpace services because of the changing nature of the increased services sought and requested by society. Research from the Council for Aid to Education (CAE) predicts a funding shortfall for higher education of $38 billion by 2015 (Benjamin, 1998). Some 3 million of the 14 million college and university students are participating in developmental education, and it seems likely that this ratio will increase, requiring even greater academic resources and public financial support to ensure their success. Far from preparing for these rising enrollments, several public policy trends are threatening such access. Perhaps the greatest threat is complacency, because steps need to be taken now to meet the changes that are almost certain to occur. The students of the future are already in the pipeline at the K–12 level.

There are numerous reasons for maintaining, even broadening, access to higher education, not the least of them practical and economic. Current figures indicate that a college graduate earns approximately $1 million more over his or her lifetime than a high school graduate. Not only will this student pay a greater amount in taxes, rather than being a tax burden, but will be less likely to end up a prisoner and more likely to participate in civic activities, such as voting. Failed education as well as failure to secure an education is an extravagant waste of public resources and ultimately costs both the public and the participant more. A contemporary slogan gets right to the point: "If you think education is expensive, try ignorance." The states average $21,000 a year on each prisoner, who pays no taxes and has a high recidivism rate. Welfare expenditures total some $250 billion a year by the most conservative estimates (Silber, 1998).

If we can alter an individual's life from being on welfare or in prison, to becoming a tax-paying, self-reliant citizen, we improve our own lot as well as extend the democratic concepts of excellence, fairness, justice, and equal opportunity. It is hard to imagine a more desirable future course of action, or a more contentious one.

## References

Balderston, F. E. *Managing Today's University: Strategies for Viability, Change, and Excellence.* (2nd ed.) San Francisco: Jossey-Bass, 1995.

Benjamin, R. "Looming Deficits: Causes, Consequences, and Cures." *Change,* 1998, *30*(2), 12–17.

California Citizens Commission on Higher Education. *Toward a State of Learning.* Final Report. Los Angeles: Citizens Commission on Higher Education, Mar. 1999.

Cohen, A. M. *The Shaping of American Higher Education: Emergence and Growth of the Contemporary System.* San Francisco: Jossey-Bass, 1998.

Layzell, D. T., and Caruthers, J. K. "Budget and Budget-Related Policy Issues for Multicampus Systems." In G. Gaither (ed.), *The Multicampus System: Perspectives on Practice and Prospects.* Sterling, Va.: Stylus, 1999.

Silber, J. "Good Teachers Deserve a Tax Break." *Wall Street Journal,* Oct. 5, 1998, p. A30.

*GERALD H. GAITHER is director of institutional effectiveness, research, and analysis at the Prairie View A&M University campus of the Texas A&M University System.*

9

*The materials cited in this chapter are largely available through the new electronic technologies and are based on recent scholarship. They provide a cogent collection of practical sources for dealing with each of the topics of recruitment, remediation, and retention.*

# Recruitment, Remediation, and Retention: Suggestions for Further Reading and Research

*Anthony J. Adam*

The literature of recruitment, remediation, and retention is vast—far greater than the scope of this brief guide to further reading and research could hope to approach. The following items are generally broad in their approach toward these issues; a quick ERIC search will retrieve numerous localized articles and reports. I have therefore selected the resources I believe will be most fruitful to the greatest number of researchers. I also emphasize resources appearing since 1997, because they will provide their own secondary bibliographies, although significant older studies could not be omitted. In addition, I have mixed the theoretical with the practical throughout, and I hope that readers will find a variety of perspectives that will stimulate debate and additional research. The Web sites, of course, might disappear completely with time, that being the nature of the World Wide Web. The bibliography subdivides among the Three Rs, but it is not unusual for a resource to discuss two of the three simultaneously. Note also that the chapters in this volume have cited other valuable resources.

## Recruitment

Eaglin, R., Osborne, J. S., and Seelig, M. *Comparison of Public and Private Campus CEO Involvement in Student Recruitment and Retention Activities.* Washington, D.C.: American Association of State Colleges and Universities, 1999. Available at http://www.aascu.org/analysis/presidents-recruitment /download.pdf (accessed Feb. 23, 1999). As enrollment issues become more significant to a university's success, the role of the campus president grows more complex. Morehead State President Eaglin's survey reports that although a large percentage of presidents indicated they had directed a strategic planning effort on enrollment development, there were differences between public and private sectors on the effectiveness of this strategy. Also, lines of reporting between presidents and chief enrollment officers vary significantly between public and private institutions. This is an excellent large survey (of twelve hundred campuses) on current practices that will be of interest to all institutional enrollment managers and presidents. (This report is entitled "The Role of College Presidents in Recruitment and Retention" on the Web page; the title provided here is from .pdf document.)

*GEAR UP: Gaining Early Awareness and Readiness for Undergraduate Programs.* Washington, D.C.: U.S. Department of Education, 1998. Available at http://www.ed.gov/gearup/ (accessed Feb. 2, 1999). Created by the Higher Education Amendments of 1998 (Public Law 105-244), GEAR UP provides partnership and state grants to support early college preparation and awareness activities at the local and state levels. As of this writing, no grants have been awarded, but the Web site does include brief examples of mentoring and early awareness programs in action, such as Project GRAD in Houston and George Mason University's Early Identification Program. The Web page on "Resources to Help Plan GEAR UP Projects" is especially useful for its links to Department of Education and other programs. Educators should also visit the Department of Education's "Think College Early" Web site at http://www.ed.gov/thinkcollege/early/ for additional mentoring and preparation suggestions.

Gehring, D. D. (ed.). *Responding to the New Affirmative Action Climate.* New Directions for Student Services, no. 83. San Francisco: Jossey-Bass, 1998. With race-preferential college admissions lawsuits either recently concluded or pending in the Fifth District Court, Washington State, California, Michigan, and elsewhere, all admissions officers would do well to read through this volume for background. After a brief historical overview of affirmative action, the volume focuses on specific issues. Kolling clarifies current legal opinion relating to admissions policies, with special reference to Proposition 209, while Scott and Kibler examine the *Hopwood* decision and its effects. Finally, Shuford offers practical suggestions to help admissions and other campus professionals to increase diversity.

Horn, L. J., and Berktold, J. *Profile of Undergraduates in U.S. Postsecondary Education Institutions: 1995–96,* with an essay on: Undergraduates Who Work, NCES 98-084. Washington, D.C.: National Center for Education Statistics, 1998. Available at http://nces.ed.gov/pubs98/98084.html (accessed Oct. 4, 1998). Four of five undergraduates reported working while enrolled in college, and 29 percent considered themselves primarily employees taking classes in their spare time. This report focuses on the characteristics of these students, including grade point average, attendance, financial aid, and educational aspirations. Table 7.2 tabulates the percentage of first- and second-year students who took remedial classes.

Kane, T. J., and Dickens, W. T. *Racial and Ethnic Preference in College Admissions*. Brookings Policy Brief 9. Nov. 1996. Available at http://www.brookings .org/comm/PolicyBriefs/pb009/pb9.htm (accessed Nov. 17, 1998). The authors examine the evidence on the true extent of racial preference in college admissions and its impact on the careers of the intended beneficiaries to determine the future of race-based admissions policies in a post–Proposition 209 world. The end of racial preferences will have little effect on the college plans of high school seniors, the authors argue, as preferences in admissions policies are strong primarily at elite universities and less so at those with SAT admissions scores below the top 20 percent.

*Knocking at the College Door: Projections of High School Graduates by State and Race/Ethnicity, 1996–2012.* Boulder, Colo.: Western Interstate Commission for Higher Education, 1998. This joint publication by the Western Interstate Commission for Higher Education and the College Board, essential for any enrollment manager, projects a rising tide of high school graduates through the year 2008, followed by a sharp decline, with a decrease in Anglo graduates offset by a slight increase among Hispanics and Asian Americans. The complete data set, available in both paper and CD-ROM, provides breakdowns of graduates by race, by state, and by year.

*Miles to Go: A Report on Black Students and Postsecondary Education in the South.* Atlanta, Ga.: Southern Education Foundation, 1998. An analysis of the status of African Americans in public higher education in the nineteen states that at one time operated dual systems of public higher education. Following recent legal decisions on racial preferences in admissions, higher education systems in many of these states are raising performance standards, including admission requirements, for all students, regardless of race, and moves are afoot throughout the nation to eliminate remedial programs at four-year institutions, with mixed success. This glossy report, funded in part by the Ford, Rockefeller, and Coca-Cola foundations, presents numerous charts detailing higher education trends by race, in addition to excellent summaries of the current legal status and promising practices of each state.

Nelsen, A. K., and others. *Crucial Practices for Diversity: A Project Report.* University Park, Pa.: Alliance for Undergraduate Education, 1994. (ED 385 800) With the cooperation of a group of large public universities, Alliance for Undergraduate Education (AUE) researchers conducted on-site visits and identified nine crucial practices for retaining undergraduate students of color: vision, diversity, centralization versus decentralization, leadership, communication, data, accountability, coordination of retention and recruitment programs, and commitment capital. Each of these areas is discussed briefly in terms of its application to the contemporary campus. However, in striving for diversity, an institution must foremost examine and deal with its values, structures, and processes openly, seriously, and positively. The AUE team argues that although resources are often on hand, the administrative will is lacking to achieve success.

Orfield, G., and Miller, E. (eds.). *Chilling Admissions: The Affirmative Action Crisis and the Search for Alternatives.* Cambridge, Mass.: Harvard Education Publishing Group, 1998. This first monograph from the Harvard Civil Rights Project addresses the central issues of minority admissions at universities subject to the aftermath of California's Proposition 209 and the *Fordice* and *Hopwood* decisions. Although the nine chapters focus primarily on California, Texas, and Mississippi, admissions officers throughout the United States will find much useful information here for post–affirmative action policymaking.

*Plan 2008: Educational Quality Through Racial/Ethnic Diversity.* Madison: Office of Multicultural Affairs, University of Wisconsin System Administration, 1998. Available at http://www.uwsa.edu/multcult/reports.htm (accessed Mar. 30, 1999). Launched in 1988, the University of Wisconsin system Design for Diversity plan established goals to increase enrollment of targeted students of color throughout the system by 100 percent in ten years. However, the system reported only a 48.5 percent increase among this group, for an 11.3 percent total nonwhite enrollment (or 7.7 percent native-born students) in fall 1997. Step Two, labeled Plan 2008, seeks to increase the number of well-prepared high school graduates of color who apply to the system in order to bring enrollment, retention, and graduation rates for these students into alignment with those of the student body as a whole.

Stringer, W. L., and others. *It's All Relative: The Role of Parents in College Financing and Enrollment.* Washington, D.C.: Institute for Higher Education Policy, 1998. Available at http://www.usagroup.com/pdfs/merisoti.pdf (accessed Jan. 20, 1991). One major element of recruitment and enrollment that has received scant consideration is the role of the parent. This study demonstrates that although parents remain committed to financing their children's education, their support covers diminishing amounts of the total cost. Roughly two-thirds of parents use current income to pay for college costs, with the remaining third borrowing or dipping into savings. Parents participate significantly in the enrollment process also by talking with university personnel, filling out applications, and discussing curriculum.

Swann, C. C., and Henderson, S. E. (eds.). *Handbook of the College Admissions Profession.* Westport, Conn.: Greenwood Press, 1998. Written primarily as a guidebook for new enrollment managers, the handbook examines the entire admissions process in nineteen chapters written by academic professionals. Individual chapters study the historical background of admissions and recruitment; admissions as a career, including the role of professional associations, training, and ethics; strategic enrollment management; admissions tools, including developing a marketing plan, applying technology, writing policies and procedures, and recruitment practices; admissions programs for specialized groups; telecounseling and recruitment videos; and a consideration of the student of the future. This is an essential resource for anyone involved in admissions and recruitment.

## Remediation

Boylan, H. R., and others. "The Historical Roots of Developmental Education." *Research in Developmental Education,* 1987/1988, 4(4–5), 5(3). (ED 341 434) This three-part article appeared in the official newsletter of the National Center for Developmental Education at Appalachian State University (see below). Part I, "Educating All the People" (Boylan and W. G. White, Jr.), covers the seventeenth-century beginnings of developmental education in the United States through the founding of colleges for women and African Americans. Part II, "Historically Black Colleges and Universities: A Force in Developmental Education" (H. Jones and H. Richards-Smith), focuses on the significance of historically black colleges and universities for African American higher education. Part III, "The Historical Roots of Developmental Education" (Boylan), brings the story to the present. The article provides a good summation of forces leading to contemporary problems and issues.

Breneman, D. W., and Haarlow, W. N. "Remedial Education: Costs and Consequences." *Fordham Report,* July 1998, 2(9). Available at http://www.edexcellence.net/library/remed.html (accessed Oct. 4, 1998). Breneman, a former Brookings Institution economist specializing in higher education, examines the remediation question from a budgetary standpoint. He concludes that although remediation absorbs $1 billion annually of a $115 billion public higher education budget, that cost is minimal compared to the alternative of dead-end jobs, welfare, and unemployment. Robert Costrell's accompanying commentary on nonbudgetary costs adds a further dimension to this excellent report. This is an expanded version of Breneman, "Remediation in Higher Education: Its Extent and Cost," *Brookings Papers on Education Policy 1998* (Washington, D.C.: Brookings Institution), 359–383.

Creech, J. D. *Better Preparation, Less Remediation: Challenging Courses Make a Difference.* Atlanta, Ga.: Southern Regional Education Board, 1997. Available at http://www.sreb.org/main/latestreports/accountbench/remediation/remediation.html (accessed 10/20/98). This brief document focuses on the front end of the higher education remediation problem: the quality of high school education. To prepare potential freshmen better, states must require students to meet a higher academic standard, especially in mathematics courses, which should then eliminate the need for much remediation, although some will be necessary for adults who do not move directly from high school to college and thus need to improve their basic skills.

Dwinell, P. L., and Higbee, J. L. (eds.). *Developmental Education and Its Role in Preparing Successful College Students.* Columbia, S.C.: National Resource Center for the First-Year Experience and Students in Transition, 1998. This joint publication of FYE and the National Association for Developmental Education examines the history, current status, and future of developmental education in U.S. universities. Emphasis is placed on the need for diversity and equity in higher education. This book, a well-written guide for all college-level developmental education practitioners, discusses many practical applications of developmental education, including the needs to integrate skill development with course content and the effectiveness of strategic learning, personal management training, and supplemental instruction.

Ignash, J. M. (ed.). *Implementing Effective Policies for Remedial and Developmental Education.* New Directions for Community Colleges, no. 100. San Francisco: Jossey-Bass, 1997. As states and university systems seek to eliminate developmental education from higher education, the burden will fall to community colleges to help students make the successful transition from high school to university. The chapters examine a variety of issues relative to remediation, including mandatory placement and assessment, open access policies, financial aid, quality versus quantity in program delivery for English as a Second Language students, current practices, evaluation methods for remedial programs, and community college–high school feedback and collaboration.

Lewis, L., and Farris, E. *Remedial Education at Higher Education Institutions in Fall 1995.* NCES 97-584. Washington, D.C.: National Center for Education Statistics, 1996. Available at http://nces.ed.gov/pubs/97584.pdf (accessed Oct. 4, 1998). Data collected in fall 1995 from two-year and four-year higher education institutions that enroll freshmen show that 78 percent of the institutions offered at least one remedial course, two-year institutions offered more remedial courses than four-year institutions, and most students do not take lengthy remedial courses. The final report includes data on retention rates, reasons institutions do not offer remedial programs, and state and other policies and laws affecting remedial education. An earlier survey, *College-Level Remedial Education in the Fall of 1989*, NCES 91-191 (NCES, 1991; available at http://nces.ed.gov/pubs91/91191.pdf), and *Indicator of the Month: Remedial Education in Higher Education Institutions*, NCES 98-004 (NCES, 1998; available at http://nces.ed.gov/pubs/ce/c97p26.pdf), are highly useful comparative pieces.

McCabe, R. H., and Day, P. R. (eds.). *Developmental Education: A Twenty-First Century Social and Economic Imperative.* Laguna Hills, Calif.: League for Innovation in the Community College, 1998. (ED 421 176) Although the target audience is primarily community college personnel, administrators at the university level will find much of interest also. After a historical overview of the importance of developmental education in American society, chapters turn to "Work, the Individual, and the Economy," "What Works in Developmental Education," and "The Case for Developmental Education in the Twenty-First Century," all of which demonstrate the importance of remedial programs in maintaining a healthy economy both now and in the future. Finally, ten community colleges describe their exemplary developmental programs.

Miller, K. J. *Developmental Education at the College Level. Fastback 404.* Bloomington, Ind.: Phi Delta Kappa, 1996. (ED 405 763) This brief introductory guide to remedial education outlines the fundamental nature of developmental education. Developmental students are normally poor choosers of high school course work, adult learners, nonnative speakers of English, students with disabilities, or students with undefined goals. Thus, remedial education includes classes and programs designed to fit a variety of needs. Ultimately, students who go through remedial programs graduate from college at nearly the same rate as nonremedial students, thus justifying the programs.

National Association for Developmental Education Web site home page. Available at http://www.umkc.edu/cad/nade/index.htm (accessed Mar. 24, 1999). The National Association for Developmental Education (NADE) seeks to improve the theory and practice of developmental education in postsecondary education through strengthening professional abilities and designing programs to match student needs. Particularly useful are the links to full-text NADE monographs and selected conference papers, policy statements and other documents by NADE leaders, and selected articles from the journal *Research and Teaching in Developmental Education* (New York College Learning Skills Association).

National Center for Developmental Education Web site home page. Available at http://www.ced.appstate.edu/centers/ncde/ (accessed Mar. 25, 1999). Centered at the Reich College of Education at Appalachian State University, the National Center for Developmental Education (NCDE) provides instruction, training, and contracted research on underprepared college students and sponsors the *Journal of Developmental Education* and the Kellogg Institute for the Training and Certification of Developmental Educators. Unfortunately, most of the information listed at this Web site must be ordered from the center rather than downloaded. Most useful as the contact point for Boylan (see above), Dr. Barbara S. Bonham, and other developmental education researchers.

Phipps, R. *College Remediation: What It Is, What It Costs, What's at Stake.* Washington, D.C.: Institute for Higher Education Policy, 1998. Available at http://www.ihep.com/Remediation.pdf (accessed Dec. 2, 1998). In response to recent reports castigating remedial programs, this Institute for Higher Education Policy (IHEP) work argues that remediation is a necessary component of higher education and should remain so, partly because there is little agreement as to what constitutes "college-level" work. There is also no evidence that remedial programs are growing at U.S. universities; moreover, the modest costs are comparable to or lower than other campus programs. Ultimately remedial programs are a benefit to society in that they track students away from unemployment and low-paying jobs.

Russell, A. B. *Statewide College Admissions, Student Preparation, and Remediation Policies and Programs: Summary of a 1997 SHEEO Survey.* Denver: Organization of State Higher Education Executive Officers, 1998. This reports the findings of a fifty-state survey of higher education coordinating and governing boards on initiatives directed toward college admissions policies and practices and college remediation policies. It focuses partly on changes to admissions standards and state and board initiatives to improve or eliminate remediation policies. Summary articles were published in *Network News: A Quarterly Bulletin of the SHEEO/NCES Communication Network,* 1998, 17(2) (available at http://www.sheeo.org/SHEEO/network/nn-index.htm).

Webliography for Developmental Educators. Available at http://www.schooledu.swt.edu/Dev.ed/Technology/Webliography.html (accessed Mar. 24, 1999). This provides a variety of links to professional organizations specific to developmental education, those focusing on developmental education research, select learning centers and writing labs on the World Wide Web, links connected with distance education, and student study strategy information. Many of the links are no longer valid, but there are still enough useful active sites to merit a visit. The Research section links to the *Education Policy Analysis Archives* (http://olam.ed.asu.edu/epaa/), an education journal based at Arizona State University that addresses numerous higher education issues.

## Retention

American Association for State Colleges and Universities/Sallie Mae National Retention Project. Washington, D.C.: American Association for State Colleges and Universities, 1997. Available at http://www.aascu.org/specialreports/97/retention/ (accessed Mar. 15, 1999). Since 1992, the American Association for State Colleges and Universities has surveyed member institutions to collect information on their six-year graduation rates for full-time students and to access factors relative to graduation and retention. Using Richardson's and Tinto's studies of campus culture and retention, the National Retention Project focused on the institution rather than the students. Generally it learned that institutions with higher admission criteria achieved higher graduation rates, but also that historically black colleges and universities report higher minority student graduation rates than do colleges and universities that are not historically black. Findings are reported and graphed.

Astin, A. W. *What Matters in College: Four Critical Years Revisited.* San Francisco: Jossey-Bass, 1993. This update of Astin's seminal book on undergraduate life in the United States (*Four Critical Years,* 1977) discusses the myriad factors that affect student selection of a campus, success during the college career, and what keeps them there until graduation. Educators and policymakers will note correlations between high school and college grade point average, faculty-student ratio, student involvement in various activities (including drinking), and overall satisfaction with the college environment. This book is vital for anyone interested in undergraduate retention.

Collegeways Home Page. Available at http://www.collegeways.com (accessed Nov. 11, 1998). Primarily the work of Alan Seidman, assistant vice president for enrollment management at West Chester University in West Chester, Pennsylvania, this site hosts a number of important works that focus on college retention issues. It presents a lengthy unannotated bibliography of retention resources, from the 1970s to the present, and basic subscription information for the forthcoming *Journal of College Student Retention* supplement access to retention-l, Seidman's listserv open to practitioners and the general community (by subscription). The Publications segment features a few full-text articles by Seidman on retention.

Eimers, M. T., and Pike, G. R. "Minority and Nonminority Adjustment to College: Differences or Similarities?" *Research in Higher Education,* 1997, *38*(1), 77–97. Acknowledging that African American and Hispanic students are more likely to drop out than their white counterparts, the authors studied whether such factors as parental encouragement and student-faculty interaction significantly affect college student retention. Applying the results of a survey at a midwestern public research university to a standard retention model, Eimers and Pike determined that there are few substantive differences in the college adjustment process between minority and nonminority students.

Johnson, M. M., and Molnar, D. "Comparing Retention Factors for Anglo, Black, and Hispanic Students." Paper presented at the Association for Institutional Research Annual Conference, Albuquerque, May 1996. (ED 410 774)

Three thousand new undergraduate students at Barry University (Florida) were studied and surveyed from 1991 to 1995 to determine what factors influenced retention rates. The research team compared standardized test scores, students' academic performance at their previous institution, and academic performance at Barry. First-year grade point average, regardless of ethnicity, had the most profound effect on retention rates, contributing roughly 81 percent to a predictive retention model. Variables interacting with ethnicity had only a 7 percent impact on retention. Only African American and Hispanic grade point averages were affected by student satisfaction with academic support (such as outside class help). Financial difficulties affected retention only for resident alien students.

National Commission on the Cost of Higher Education. *Straight Talk About College Costs and Prices*. Washington, D.C.: U.S. Government Printing Office, 1998. Available at http://www.house.gov/eeo/collcost.pdf (accessed Feb. 18, 1999). Established through Public Law 105-18 as an advisory body charged with reviewing the broad issue of college costs and prices, the commission reported that institutions, parents, and other parties share responsibility in containing college expense. However, tuition price controls would not work; rather, they would be destructive of the high academic quality of higher education. To avoid increased federal cost-control regulation, the commission recommends shared responsibility to strengthen institutional cost control, rethink accreditation, and improve market information and public accountability. Because this report is designed especially for wide public consumption, enrollment managers and campus presidents studying recruitment issues would best take note of these recommendations.

National Resource Center for the First-Year Experience and Students in Transition. Available at http://www.sc.edu/fye/ (accessed Mar. 23, 1999). Chartered in 1986 and based at the University of South Carolina, FYE (as it is known) collects and disseminates information about the first college year and other significant student transitions. This Web site includes information on University 101, the University of South Carolina seminar class for new students that introduces them to campus life; University 401, the capstone program for seniors; teleconferences and meetings; an on-line publication and audiovisual resource catalog; and links to resources on the first-year experience. The center also publishes *Journal of the Freshman Year Experience and Students in Transition* and *Freshman Year Experience Newsletter*. The Web site is an excellent starting point for all retention and recruitment issues, with some material on remediation.

Obiakor, F. E., and Harris-Obiakor, P. *Retention Models for Minority College Students*. Emporia, Kans.: Emporia State University, 1997. (ED 406 907) Four phases are critical to the retention and achievement of minority students. In "acceptance," the college must convince the minority students that it is interested in them and wants them to succeed. "Acclimatization" builds a positive racial climate and outlines clearly stated retention policies. It is also the "responsibility" of campus minority leaders to conduct leadership workshops for these students, with a focus on conducting meetings and effective leadership practices. Finally, "productivity" means that the campus minority leadership milieu must destroy stereotypes that hinder the progress and success of minority students.

*Policies and Practices: A Focus on Higher Education Retention.* Washington, D.C.: American Association for State Colleges and Universities, 1997. (ED 421 045) Based on a discussion at a February 1995 interactive American Association for State Colleges and Universities (AASCU) videoconference, Retention Strategies for Campus Diversity, this monograph examines general student retention strategies and diversity issues in the context of the AASCU/Sallie Mae National Retention Project. The eight chapters include coverage of the AASCU/SMNRP partnership; an examination of systematic retention strategies at the local and system levels; the role of the university president in retention; and the relationship between academic advising and retention. It includes an excellent lengthy secondary bibliography.

*Recruitment and Retention in Higher Education.* $217 annual subscription. Available in both paper and diskette format. This ten-page monthly newsletter provides short articles and reports for faculty and administrators seeking answers to their recruitment and retention problems. It also features a regular column of advice from experts and book reviews. Although expensive for an education-related publication, the quality of information is worth the price.

Seidman, A. J. (ed.) *Journal of College Student Retention: Research, Theory and Practice.* Quarterly. $40 individuals, $110 institutional subscriptions. Alan Seidman, author of a popular college retention Web site (See Collegeways Home Page above), intends this new peer-reviewed journal to provide the educational community, government officials, and the general public a medium to explore retention and attrition issues. The inaugural issue includes articles on predicting retention from students' experiences with college processes; the use of reflexive photography in the study of the freshman-year experience; research on alternative admission criteria; and African American underrepresentation at the doctoral level. Although retention articles appear regularly in the academic press, this journal is a welcome addition to the literature of educational administration.

*Ten Strategies and Their Financial Implications for Reducing Time-to-Degree in Texas Universities.* Austin: Division of Research, Planning and Finance, Texas Higher Education Coordinating Board, 1996. Available at http://www .thecb.state.tx.us/divisions/planning/degree/toc.htm (accessed Oct. 27,

1998). The percentage of Texas undergraduates who completed their degree programs in four years or less declined from 45.4 percent in 1977 to 31.1 percent in 1990. Long times to graduation increase costs to the state, students, and parents and negatively affect retention rates. This report briefly describes ten strategies for reducing time to degree, including reducing credits required for graduation and using distance education and technology, with the advantages and disadvantages of each strategy. No one strategy is finally recommended.

Terrell, M. C., and Wright, D. J. (eds.). *From Survival to Success: Promoting Minority Student Retention.* Washington, D.C.: National Association of Student Personnel Administrators, 1988. (ED 335 999) This collection focuses particularly on minority student retention. Writers cover such issues as the moral and legal imperative of minority student retention; the historical background of the issue; social and psychological factors affecting retention; the emergence of multicultural centers on predominantly white campuses; factors relative to the academic success of minority students and suggested models for improvement of advisement services; and the future of minority retention. Much of this material can be found elsewhere, although the essay on multicultural centers is interesting, if now dated.

Tinto, V. *Leaving College: Rethinking the Causes and Cures of Student Attrition.* (2nd ed.) Chicago: University of Chicago Press, 1993. Vincent Tinto has long been one of the leading theorists of college student retention. In this revision of his 1987 seminal study, he argues that institutions must be strongly committed to quality education and the building of campus social community if retention is to occur. The book examines patterns of student attrition, addresses the roots of individual departure and reasons that those students fail to become part of the institution's social life, and studies what actions institutions can take to prevent attrition. The lengthy secondary bibliography makes this book a primary research tool for those interested in retention issues.

Upcraft, M. L., and others. *The Freshman Year Experience: Helping Students Survive and Succeed in College.* San Francisco: Jossey-Bass, 1989. This seminal collection is basic reading for all college administrators, student affairs professionals, and others involved particularly in the retention of freshman students. The five parts study the retention problem from a number of angles: what makes the 1990s incoming student different from past entrants; how campuses can foster freshman success, including wellness programs, activities, and counseling and mentoring; the importance of the freshman seminar and how to make it a significant experience for both the student and teacher; the diversity issue, including the need to address the needs of ethnic groups, women, nontraditional students, and honors students; and building alliances between student affairs professionals and teaching faculty, an area too often neglected on most campuses. A brief but excellent secondary bibliography concludes this important work.

*ANTHONY J. ADAM is reference librarian in the J. B. Coleman Library at Prairie View A&M University, Prairie View, Texas.*

# INDEX

# Back Issue/Subscription Order Form

Copy or detach and send to:
**Jossey-Bass Inc., Publishers, 350 Sansome Street, San Francisco CA 94104-1342**

Call or fax toll free!
**Phone 888-378-2537 6AM-5PM PST; Fax 800-605-2665**

Back issues:     Please send me the following issues at $23 each.
(Important: please include series initials and issue number, such as HE90.)

1. HE  _____

_____

_____

$ _____  Total for single issues

$ _____  Shipping charges (for single issues *only;* subscriptions are exempt
from shipping charges): Up to $30, add $5$^{50}$ • $30$^{01}$–$50, add $6$^{50}$
$50$^{01}$–$75, add $7$^{50}$ • $75$^{01}$–$100, add $9 • $100$^{01}$–$150, add $10
Over $150, call for shipping charge.

Subscriptions     Please ❑ start   ❑ renew my subscription to *New Directions
for Higher Education* for the year _____ at the following rate:

❑ Individual $58        ❑ Institutional $104
**NOTE:** Subscriptions are quarterly, and are for the calendar year only.
Subscriptions begin with the spring issue of the year indicated above.
For shipping outside the U.S., please add $25.

$ _____  Total single issues and subscriptions (CA, IN, NJ, NY, and DC
residents, add sales tax for single issues. NY and DC residents must
include shipping charges when calculating sales tax. NY and Canadian
residents only, add sales tax for subscriptions.)

❑ Payment enclosed (U.S. check or money order only)
❑ VISA, MC, AmEx, Discover Card #_____ Exp. date_____

Signature _____ Day phone _____

❑ Bill me (U.S. institutional orders only. Purchase order required.)
Purchase order #_____

Name _____

Address _____

_____

_____

Phone_____ E-mail _____

For more information about Jossey-Bass Publishers, visit our Web site at:
www.josseybass.com                    **PRIORITY CODE = ND1**